THE

FUTURE

OF

GERMANY

BY

KARL JASPERS

Translated and Edited by E. B. Ashton
with a Foreword by Hannah Arendt

The University of Chicago Press

CHICAGO AND LONDON

This translation of "Aspekte der Bundesrepublik"—the third and main part, dealing with German political developments and prospects, of Karl Jaspers' *Wohin treibt die Bundesrepublik?* (1966)—has been brought up to date by incorporating in the foreign policy chapter and in the Postscript some major parts of the author's new book *Antwort: Zur Kritik meiner Schrift "Wohin treibt die Bundesrepublik?"* (1967). Both books © by R. Piper & Co. Verlag, Munich.

Library of Congress Catalog Card Number: 67-25510

THE UNIVERSITY OF CHICAGO PRESS, CHICAGO & LONDON
The University of Toronto Press, Toronto 5, Canada

FOREWORD

A book by Karl Jaspers needs no introduction by me or by anybody else. However, a few words may not be out of place in this particular case in order to prepare the American reader for the rather astounding fact that a philosopher, and a German philosopher to boot, should have written the politically most important book to appear in Germany after the Second World War. Moreover, its main thesis must come as a shock to the American public: that the Federal Republic of West Germany is well on its way to abolishing parliamentary democracy and may be drifting toward some kind of dictatorship which under certain conditions—if, for example, Germany should decide to follow de Gaulle and withdraw its armed forces from NATO—could become a threat to peace in Europe.

For in our preoccupation with this country's new enterprises in Asia, we have paid little attention to rather frightening signs of disintegration in Europe, particularly in Germany, and

we have received even less information about them. And to the
extent that correspondents and magazine writers were breaking
this wall of ignorance and silence, it was, with very few exceptions, to tell us not to worry—Bonn is not Weimar; a
resurgence of nationalism is only natural; the fact that the new
chancellor is a former high-ranking official of Ribbentrop's
Foreign Office is a healthy sign for Germany's political recovery, for his vice chancellor is a Socialist and former refugee,
and the two together make "a good example for the unification
of the nation" (Willy Brandt); the recent election sucesses of
the National Democratic Party (NPD), an extremist right-
wing group, which nobody had foreseen, should give no cause
for alarm although greater successes are expected in the near
future; serious anti-Semitic incidents in the armed forces,
where the NPD is especially strong among the lower echelons
of the officer corps, were hardly reported in Germany and not
at all in this country; nor, so far as I know, did our newspapers
see fit to print the reaction of Franz Josef Straus, Bonn's new
minister of finance, to the electoral success of the NDP, "This
is the answer to the years when everything German and all
national sentiments were dragged through the mud." It is well
known, on the other hand, that West Germany has never recognized the Oder-Neisse line, that no party has ever dared to
declare publicly that such recognition of the status quo in the
East was part of its program, and that claims to the lost eastern territories have grown in intensity during the past years;
but these alarming cries of outrage should not be taken seriously,
we are told, because tacitly and privately all this, including the
existence of two German states, has long been accepted in Bonn.
Each of these counsels of complacency has been refuted in
print inside as well as outside Germany, but the spell of
complacency was never broken. Not even the cries of a "second
Versailles," with which the negotiations between this country
and the Soviet Union about an agreement of non-proliferation

of atomic weapons were greeted by large strata of German public and official opinion—certainly the most alarming symptom of the changed mood in the *Bundesrepublik*—were thought significant enough to be properly reported.

This book sounds the alarm. When Jaspers wrote it, about two years ago, and when it was published more than a year ago, much of the evidence I have quoted above had not yet materialized. Hence, it is only now—in his just-published "Answer to My Critics," of which certain parts have been incorporated into the American edition—when faced with the accomplished fact of the "great coalition," namely, the de facto elimination of parliamentary opposition, with the imminence of an emergency law (*Notstandsgesetzgebung*), which would in effect annul the constitution, and with the emergence of an aggressive new party, which "reveals the bankruptcy of the rest" and fills provisionally the vacuum in Bonn ("the craziest faith may spread in such a situation"), that he sums up the inescapable conclusion of all his analyses—"A new moral-political catastrophe may be in store for us."

Jaspers does not believe in a revival of Nazism, and under present circumstances this is indeed quite unlikely, although some of the spokesmen for the new NDP said publicly that not Hitler but international Jewry was to be blamed for the outbreak of the last war. Bonn may not be Weimar, but the disintegration processes in the Bonn government show traits conspicuously similar to those that characterized the last months of the Weimar Republic. Who can help being reminded of Brüning's ill-fated *Notverordnungen* of 1931 when he hears of *Notstandsgesetze?* And the fact that, in contrast to the economic and political crisis of the early thirties, there exists no emergency at all this time, as Jaspers points out, is not reassuring; on the contrary, one has the impression that this perfectly superfluous enterprise uses an allegedly possible emergency merely as a pretext to get rid of the present form of govern-

ment. The difference is only that "the very threat which in the
Weimar Republic came from anti-state forces in search of revolutionary change lies now in the state itself. It is not menaced
by countermovements. No opposition transforms it. It transforms itself, vaguely pursuing the very aims that were pursued
in those days: authority, authoritarian state, dictatorship."

Historically speaking, it is undeniable that the Bonn government was established as a conscious attempt to create not a
"new state" but the *status quo ante* Hitler, that is, a restoration
of the Weimar Republic. The constitutional changes in the
new Basic Law, as the Bonn constitution is generally called, are
technical devices destined to amend certain institutional short-
comings which were blamed by experts in constitution-making
for the disaster in 1933. Hence the cliché "Bonn is not Weimar." (How Bonn may well be on its way to "becoming
Weimar" has just been explained in detail by Karl Dietrich
Bracher, Germany's foremost historian of the "disintegration
of the Weimar Republic," in an article in *Der Spiegel*.) It is
frequently forgotten today that in the crisis of 1932 there
existed an alternative to Nazi rule, and this was a military
dictatorship under General Schleicher, whom the Nazis, well
aware of this possibility, promptly assassinated. Should Jaspers'
fears that the West German government may drift into a military dictatorship come true, it would be almost the proof—if
proof in such matters were possible—that Bonn is indeed the
repeat performance of Weimar which it was meant to be from
its very beginnings.

With an unfailing eye for the essential, Jaspers passes quickly
over the last twenty years of German history, and in evaluating
it he has the great advantage of remembering vividly and concretely the whole span of twentieth-century history. He was
thirty years old when the First World War broke out in an
atmosphere of nationalist paroxysm, and he watched at close
quarters the second paroxysm twenty years later when almost

the whole nation went Nazi. He is painfully aware of all that
has remained constant, not in the circumstances of the world
but in the inner condition and the behavior of the people. This
is not a question of an eternal German national character; it
is a matter of typical and repeated behavior patterns ever since
Bismarck founded the German Reich. The danger now lies in
the automatic consequences of the fact that "no new state
emerged in 1945," and that no clear break with the past, not
even the Nazi past, was ever achieved. In its stead there has
spread a general "mendacity [that] pervades our political existence, and thus our personal one," the crucial lie since the
beginnings of the Adenauer administration being "that the
Germans were never really Nazis." The great coalition, established under the mutual congratulations of the politicians and
applauded almost unanimously inside and outside Germany, is
actually the grotesque transformation of a two-party system
into a new form of government, a kind of two-party dictatorship, or, in Jaspers' words, a "dictatorship of politicians."
   In order to understand that this is indeed the beginning of
the end of parliamentary democracy in Germany, one needs
only recall the argument with which Adenauer in 1949 rejected the idea of a coalition of the two great parties. Under
such circumstances, he wrote in his memoirs, "there would
not be a forceful opposition in parliament. I was afraid of the
development of an extra-parliamentary opposition on a nationalist basis, with nationalist demagogues endangering the
young state." Seventeen years later Mr. Adenauer had forgotten whatever he might have known of the functioning of
parliamentary government; thus, shortly before his death he
was not merely impressed by General de Gaulle but full of
admiration for General Franco, who after all owes his present
position in no small degree to Hitler and Mussolini. In 1967,
at any event, neither statesmen nor politicians share this obvious, common-sense concern. There are only a few lonely

voices—a philosopher, a publicist, a novelist—who seem to
understand what should be obvious to all: Karl Jaspers, Rudolf
Augstein in *Der Spiegel,* and Günter Grass, who in two des-
perately imploring letters asked Kiesinger not to accept the
chancellorship because of his Nazi past and begged Willy
Brandt, in words which curiously recall Adenauer's early argument against a government without opposition, to reconsider
a decision which would "push me and my friends into a left
corner, degrading us to a politically impotent counterpart of
the National Democratic Party. . . . The youth of our country will turn away from this state and its constitution; it will
get stuck in some left or right [extremism] as soon as this ugly
marriage has been concluded."

Complacency, optimism born of fear, and empty self-con-
gratulation may be the chief ingredients in the present official
German atmosphere; they are very far from telling the whole
story. There must be many Germans today who are not com-
placent at all; otherwise the spectacular success of this book,
on the bestseller list since publication, would be inexplicable. But even this is not too assuring. There is something
strange about this success which is not really a *succès d'estime.*
The point is not that Bonn and everybody connected with the
government have ignored the book publicly and done everything they could to discredit it and its author privately, but
that the mainstream of respectable public opinion has been
respectfully hostile—though perhaps not to the same degree as
a few years ago when Jaspers first proposed to recognize the
DDR, the government of East Germany, under certain conditions; at that time a Swiss journalist wrote that "not even
Khrushchev succeeded in touching off such a demonstration
of national consensus." The gap between the immediate success
of the book and the criticism voiced by nearly all organs of
public opinion seems to indicate that Jaspers has succeeded in
reaching many, but that these many are precisely those whose

opinions and feelings are hardly represented at all in public. One is unhappily reminded of the only other bestseller Jaspers ever wrote, of his *Geistige Situation der Zeit* (*Man in the Modern Age*) which, published in 1931, sold five editions in the short time which separated its appearance from Hitler's rise to power. Jaspers then warned of the rapid disintegration of the Weimar Republic which made Hitler's victory possible. The kind of success he then had was ominously similar: his forebodings of an imminent catastrophe were denounced by all respectable critics, and he was read by a minority that, though perhaps strong enough numerically to make itself heard, was in fact impotent—able and willing to face the all-too-obvious realities but powerless to change them.

HANNAH ARENDT

PREFACE

The people of the German Federal Republic are more prosperous than ever, except for the rarely mentioned victims of
hard luck. The majority are satisfied and eager to enjoy life
as leisure time, consumer goods, amusements, and opportunities
for travel keep increasing.

And yet there is disquiet. Is this life safe? One senses fear.
Thinking persons regard the political facts with concern.
Which way are we drifting?

German democracy is changing before our eyes. Courses
that would leave us neither free nor democratic are taken,
although the men who set them may not want to go where
they lead. These courses are not unavoidable. But it will take
a freedom-loving nation, one that is aware of itself in freedom,
to put into practice what is now only a possibility—democracy
in a republican form of free government.

How are we ruled? Who rules us? Where do our politicians

come from? What is the structure of our republic, in terms of
fact rather than of law and theory? What are the changes that
take place in the structure? Do we not seem to be moving from
democracy to an oligarchy of parties, and from there to dictatorship?

To spot trends is not to predict them. There are infinitely
many factors and incalculable accidents involved in the determination of political events. Prophets are as wrong today
as ever. We can spot trends, but whether the trends materialize
and bear out the predictions is uncertain and depends also on us.

For an observer the question is: What happens? For a pleader
it is: What ought to happen?—What do we propose to do?

Contents

I. From Democracy to an Oligarchy of Parties   1
    The goal   1
    The question of structure   2
    Are we a democracy, and in what sense?   3
    The parties   4
    Members of parliament   5
    The changing parties   7
    Institutional promotion of this change   7
    The first symptom: state financing of parties   9
    Parliament   10
    All-party government?   13
    The oligarchy of parties   14

II. From the Oligarchy to a Dictatorship   17
    "Security"   17
    Security in the constitution   17
    Whose security?   20
    Limits of security   21
    Motivations on the road to dictatorship   22
    The state of mind: authority and subject   22
    Unreadiness for political responsibility   27
    Paralysis of political thought   27
    The Communist Party ban   28

The decline of checks and balances   29
Secrecy   29
"Minimalization" of civil rights   30
Devaluation of the mind   30
Sovereignty   31
All-party government   32
Empire, Weimar Republic, and Federal Re-
   public   32
"Patriot party" vs. "liberty party"   33
The proposed emergency laws   35
The plans and their treatment   36
External emergency   37
Internal emergency   42
The inevitability of abuse   45
Distrust   47
Toward a military dictatorship   47
Emergency laws and constitution   49
Labor views and their limitations   50
Comparison with the Nazi upheaval   51
Summary   52

III. The Background   56
The origin of our republic   56
The task then and now   57
The constitution then and now   58
The basic untruth   59
The vacuum   59
The free spirit as a third force   61
Personnel policy   65
"National character"   67

IV. Possible Domestic Policies   72
The basic decision   72
Premises of change   74

     Institutions   77
       Parliament and parties; secrecy; treason;
         controls   77
       The presidency   81
       Spontaneous popular organizations   82
     Education   85
       Science and culture   85
       Freedom and authority   86
       Instruction and study   87
       Subject matter   87
       History   87
       German history   89
       Political education   90

V. The Bundeswehr   94
       The new circumstances: the new soldier; the
         pace of weapons development; global
         strategy; world war and local wars; the
         necessity for peace   95
       Changes required in the military mind:
         obedience as a way of life; freedom in the
         army; no privileged officer class   99
       The dangers: "tradition"; false pride; shield-
         ing the government from the people   100
       Knowing the problems and controlling the
         Bundeswehr   106

VI. Foreign Policy   108
      The world situation   110
       Political realities and criteria of action   111
       Changed diplomacy and final goal   113
       Provisional goals   115
       China   118

The foreign policy of small nations   122
German foreign policy   124
Territorial borders and "legal claims"   125
The principle of self-determination   128
The new premises   131
A policy of peace   137
"Security" and the United States: pros and cons; Kennedy; Vietnam; possible and impossible security; no alternative   139
Hegemony   151
Nuclear power   153
Conclusions   155

VII.   Summary and Outlook   159

Postscript 1967   163

I

FROM DEMOCRACY TO AN OLIGARCHY OF PARTIES

THE GOAL

What do we want to achieve by means of the Federal Republic? In 1944, shortly before his attempt on Hitler's life, Claus von Stauffenberg summed up the goal in one sentence: "We want a new order that will make all Germans participants in their state and will assure them right and justice." How much of this goal has been attained?

The "new order"? So far it remains an outward, institutional one not anchored in public thinking. There, in fact, disorder is on the rise.

"All Germans participants in their state"? No, most of them are still subjects of the state rather than participants in it. Every four years they choose between lists placed before them, but they do not really know what they are choosing. They have to bow—first to the party proposals, then to authorities that claim to exercise powers conferred by the electorate.

"Right and justice"? The right, to some extent, is pledged as under any government of laws, totalitarian ones included. Our basic rights are so little protected, however, that government agencies infringe them (as in the *Spiegel* case, the wiretapping case, and others) without admitting their unconstitutional practices and without providing any kind of redress. Our judges, enthroned in unimpeachability, take their time. They feel that no one else knows the law, that they are its sole administrators, that their interpretation of it is absolute. Now and then they render incomprehensible decisions. They stir up no storm of outrage at the confusing treason clauses of our penal code; they do not insist on their swift revision and clarification. As for justice, there is no more of it now than there ever was, except for a yielding to interests represented by sufficiently strong groups. Every German who is aware of this state of affairs would like to see it improve.

THE QUESTION OF STRUCTURE

This question seems easy to answer. We need only study the constitution, and there are excellent textbooks to train us in institutional thinking. But the constitution does not determine what really happens. It does not let us foresee what men will do, what the people who live in those structures will make of them.

Muddling through leads to chaos; what is constructive is the *idea* of the state as conceived by free citizens and their representatives—not as a sum of phrases learned, but as motivating reality. Chaos leads to dictatorship; translating the idea into reality leads to political freedom. Each concrete step, each government measure, each parliamentary decision or debate should serve in its way to advance the political idea as opposed to political chaos. We cannot speak so definitely about the impulses of citizens and politicians, about their guiding ideas, as about the institutions that emerge from such basic motives and consolidate them. To speak of basic motives is an act of drawing attention rather than an act of cognition or definition. It is not only a pointing out of things but an appeal to free human beings. There are two sides to any political structure: on the one hand the institutions and laws and on the other the way they actually work, owing to the human intentions behind them or to conflicting purposes for which the institutions are misused.

ARE WE A DEMOCRACY, AND IN WHAT SENSE?

The usual answer to this question seems self-evident: Yes, we are a parliamentary democracy. The constitution says so in Article 20: "All powers of government are derived from the people." But how does this look in fact? The authors of the basic law seem to have dreaded the people, for the constitution holds the people's power to a minimum. Every four years they elect the lower house of parliament, the Bundestag, from lists of persons previously chosen by the parties. This hidden primary election is the real election, the one that decides not only who goes on his party's list but who goes high enough on it to be assured of a seat in the Bundestag under our system of proportional representation. The process is an involved one, with nominations for district and state lists handled in different manners. But it is always the party organizations that control this crucial first step, never the people. To participate in the primary election, or to be nominated for it, one must have joined a party.

Party members do not have much influence on nominations either. The decisive choices are made by the party hierarchy and bureaucracy. In drawing up state lists, a party member as such has no voice at all.

To be a voter in the full sense of the word, participating from nomination to general election, you must join a party. Unless you do, you cannot complain if all you get to vote upon is what the parties hand you. You elect people who have been elected already, and your vote affects only the number of party choices who will sit in the Bundestag.

The people have only the strictly limited choice offered to them by the parties. In theory they can reject all these proposals. In reality they have to "choose" under the sway of accidental moods—politically at sea, actually at a loss.

THE PARTIES

Our political parties are organs of the people, the supposed products of free popular initiative. "The parties," says Article 21 of the constitution, "cooperate in shaping the political will of the people." But in our republic one can scarcely speak of any such thing as a shaping of the people's political will. Most people are frighteningly uninformed. The parties tell them nothing, teach them nothing, and do not spur them to think. At election time they operate with advertising techniques, and between times they consider the material interests of groups whose votes they are after.

"Their formation is free." This is true only in a formal sense. In fact, the weight of the existing parties' organization and financial resources is such as to leave any newly formed parties without much of a chance. The major parties have become independent powers.

"Their internal order must conform to democratic principles." This is actually the case. The clause would bar a totalitarian one-party system. Majority rule prevails in our parties, as opposed to parties organized on the principle of obedience to a leader.

"They must account publicly for the sources of their

funds." Whether they do this concretely, fully, and frankly is more than doubtful.

"Parties which, by their program or by the conduct of their adherents, tend to impair or abolish the libertarian democratic basic order or to endanger the existence of the Federal Republic of Germany are unconstitutional." We shall have occasion to ask whether and at what point the present conduct of our parties does in fact impair the libertarian democratic basic order and endanger the republic.

MEMBERS OF PARLIAMENT

The people cannot participate in their own government. They are governed by their elected representatives, the legislators, who in turn elect a chancellor as chief executive. We ask, first, what influence the people have, if any—and the answer is that they have exceedingly little, that even the votes they cast are not true votes but acclamatory confirmations of decisions taken by a party oligarchy. The second question is what political qualifications the legislators ought to have, and do have. This is of fateful significance. For these men provide our government. They make the vital decisions. Their committees do the spadework.

Superhuman demands are made upon such a man. From all sides he is importuned and petitioned. He has the "public relations" job of keeping in touch with his constituents. He needs to acquire expert knowledge and to reflect on great, simple, purposeful policy lines. But he is not under orders. He can freely choose his field of activity, what seems to him important at any time. His is a marvelous occupation for one who is equal to it, but ruinous for one who does not measure up.

I know only one other occupation, an entirely different one, in which men choose their tasks and freely prove themselves without direction: academic teaching. Similar excuses are made for a professor's failure in the crucial point, which is to advance truth by productive effort; he too will cite the flood of distractions, the deluge of official and social obligations, the shortage of time in the all-devouring bustle. And the true reasons are equally similar. Both the legislator and the professor fail because they lack a sense of the essential, of the rank and proportion of things—a lack not of talent but of moral character. They fail because for all their officiousness they are lazy, vain, and pleasure-bent. The great difference is that a professor's failure hurts mainly himself and may be a contributing factor in the fate of the university, whereas the legislator's failure may doom his state and his nation.

Neither the legislator nor the professor chooses his occupation, in the sense of working toward a distinct, calculable goal. Both are venturing on careers in which they can fail—and the first sign of their failure is a desire to exclude failure, to attain the job security of bureaucrats. Neither man knows regular hours or a clear division of working day and leisure time. Both are consumed by their activity, but not in overwork, mindless diligence, obtuse drudgery and toil. Calm, detached, they will get to the heart of a problem and deal with this alone. They seem like men who always have time.

There remains another difference, a radical one. The professor's freedom is uncurbed by deadlines. He can correct his mistakes. He can wait. The statesman, on the other hand, needs presence of mind at each moment. He cannot undo what he has done. The pressures of the moment, of the situation, never cease.

Statesmanship is the highest possible achievement in the ethos of free human collaboration. In any other ethos, however true and profound, man as a communal being in the world limits himself. He ignores whatever realities do not concern him, and in a worldly sense that makes him untrue. There have been amazing achievements of impregnable faith and religious martyrdom; the works of the creative spirit are glorious, as are the natural creations of living existence. But true statesmen come to feel the inexorable limits of being human and are exalted by the most sublime potentialities of living together as a whole. Their work cannot be perfect, as can art and poetry and philosophical speculation. It is the incarnation, in the constant flux of things, of our human world in time.

When we talk like this about statesmen we are merely drafting a standard with which man may take his own measure. Man himself is not the measure. This is why everyone, even the best, remains en route and cannot reach the goal.

THE CHANGING PARTIES

A change is taking place in the meaning of our parties. They were intended to be organs of the people, manifesting the popular will and in return undertaking the people's political education. Instead, they are coming to be organs of a state which itself reverts to the authoritarian way of ruling subjects. The parties should not be the state at all; but as they withdraw from the life of the people they identify themselves with the state. They used to be diverse, autonomous products of the people's limitless freedom; now they feel that they are the powers that be. The parties are the state. The state leadership rests with the oligarchy of parties. The oligarchy usurps the state.

INSTITUTIONAL PROMOTION OF THIS CHANGE

The Federal Republic was founded with the intention of assuring stable government. The people were considered dangerous; they were to play as small a part as possible. In view of the proclaimed desire for democracy they could not be excluded altogether, but their influence was restricted to the quadrennial elections. And in these elections they were treated as a voting herd, allowed to decide nothing but the percentage of the various parties' participation in government.

Stability was to be served also by the so-called "constructive vote of no confidence." The constitution provides that a parliamentary majority can oust the chancellor only if at the same time it can agree on a new chancellor. This eliminates the struggles, the false solutions for lack of a positive majority, which marked the Weimar Republic of 1919–33. In those days this condition was one of several that prepared the ground for Nazi rule—but only because the politicians failed, not because of defects in the institution. The new principle results in a paralysis of political life. It removes the risk, not for the sake of wise, responsible government, but to promote a government activity that is politically lifeless.

Nor were the people, the nominal sovereign, allowed to wield any influence by referendum. Their one chance to affect decisions comes in elections that decide nothing and merely acknowledge the existence of the oligarchy. The fateful questions are not put to the people. The people must accept the answers, frequently without noticing that anything has been decided or how.

Another stabilizing factor is the "5 per cent clause." No party which does not receive at least 5 per cent of the total vote may enter the Bundestag. This clause was not in the original basic law; it was added later. As a result, new parties can scarcely develop. In their formative stage they are barred from parliamentary activity, unable to make a debating and voting record and to project a permanent image to the population as a whole. It is another curtailment of political life, a roadblock to everything new. The clause was designed to protect the ruling parties from new parties.

The parties' monopoly on political power transforms their

role. Temptations are inherent in a position not balanced by other powers; exclusive power corrupts even when formally divided into legislative, executive, and judicial. One possible counterweight could be the federal president if he were elected by the people, equipped with potent authority, and given legal means to exert a political influence of his own. But the drafters of our constitution, in their fear of anything resembling a plebiscite, turned thumbs down upon this popular election and thus on autonomous presidential power. Our president may engage in political intrigue but not in politics. He might, of course, exalt his stature even in his present position as a representative exponent of the best in German tradition and thought, and as a dignified world figure in the performance of his ceremonial duties; but his exclusion from the struggle over political issues leaves the parties in full control and upsets the equilibrium without which political life and the self-restraint of any power tend to cease. (The parties would need to be checked and balanced on the one hand by a president and on the other by grass-roots political formations such as the "councils" of modern revolutions. As Hannah Arendt has convincingly shown, such groupings have thus far been crushed every time by the parties, even when the party organization usurped their name, as in Russia.)

THE FIRST SYMPTOM: STATE FINANCING OF PARTIES

One symptom of the parties' identification with the state, of their capturing the state instead of serving it, is a phenomenon which in the Federal Republic did not appear until lately. The parties came to be financed by the government, thus indicating that the public treasury is their treasury, that taxpayers' money is something they can dispose of by parliamentary decision, not for public purposes only but for their own. It began with a seemingly harmless federal appropriation of 5 million marks for political education. The amount was steadily increased—in 1965, at least 45 millions in federal and state funds were paid to parties—without being limited to the original purpose. Today the parties represented in the Bundestag are publicly financed against the ones that are excluded, and against any that may be newly formed. The existing three have ceased to recognize the freedom of other parties and the free formation of new ones; having come to power, they regard themselves as the only parties, and their existence a vested right irreversible by party struggles. There are to be no new parties, and any popular initiative to that end is to be thwarted. The clarifying struggle for the citizens' will and opinion that takes place in new parties is to end; the exclusively dominant parties are to be the authorities on "correct" political opinion. Their political and intellectual confusion and the level of their representatives may make them more and more obsolete, but they will stay in power.

Parties represented in the government go a step farther and use public funds to advertise their ministers and the federal chancellor. To this end they draw on funds appropriated in lump sums, perhaps for enlightenment and education. Enlightenment is identified with propaganda. Theodor Eschenburg, a writer of excellent textbooks on German political theory and practice, speaks of a rebirth of "feudalism." What does this mean? A medieval vassal would receive his fief both to administer and to use, while modern monarchs kept the treasuries of state and court apart. "Today," says Eschenburg, "the parties, some of their ministers, and many of their deputies, bosses, propagandists, and clients, tend to regard high political offices as party fiefs." One might construct a democratic feudalism, but it would not correspond to our constitution.

PARLIAMENT

The directive role of the federal parliament is becoming ambiguous. Now it may presume to interfere with the appointive power; then it may seem bent on relinquishing more and more control.

The constitution leaves cabinet appointments to the discretion of the chancellor. In fact he makes them after consulting his party and whichever other party joins the coalition that enables him to form a government; he may even commit himself to his ministerial selections before he is elected chancellor. Under the constitution he might appoint independents or even members of the opposition party, if he were going by qualification alone. But he cannot do this in practice, for the parties want to fill the jobs with their own men. The jobs are their reward for work in the campaign, the spoils that belong to the victor.

Parliamentary control is slight. No effective use is made of investigative committees with the right of subpoena. Abuses, scandals, and fundamental questions of fact are either not handled by this method of keeping the government constantly under control and conceivably putting it right—or else, when such inquiries are launched at all, they work rather as protective screens for governmental mistakes.

This became apparent in the shocking case of Admiral Heye, the Bundestag's commissioner for the Bundeswehr, our federal army. What Heye said about its antidemocratic symptoms was very serious. Even the chief of the army spoke of an hour of doubt. But the lawmakers deserted their own commissioner; they practically turned against him, too fearful of weakening the army command's authority to recognize the major problem of the army's spirit. Heye, after years of meeting with parliamentary indifference, appealed to the public. He used modern mass media—an illustrated magazine, for instance—to summarize briefly and strikingly what hardly anyone had read in his official reports. He failed to stand firm, however. He did not retract his observations or deny his goals, but he backed away from an all-out political battle. Illness is no excuse in such a case; we still do not know what so swiftly silenced the admiral after his public outcry. Did he resent the publication of things he had privately told the president of the Bundestag? Was he influenced by traditional bonds, unable to stand his isolation among his brother officers? He should not have begun in the first place. The whole affair became a sorry, doubly clouded business. Legislative instinct seems to oppose controls wherever they could be applied in earnest. The struggle to put them into practice isolates the man who tries.

From the outset there has been an antidemocratic and illiberal element at work in the minds of our politicians. Most lacking was a common ground on which parties recognize each other as instruments of the same people within the same state. Instead, the partisan struggle has been waged by impugning one another's loyalty. Kurt Schumacher, first postwar leader of the German Social Democratic Party, called Konrad Adenauer the "chancellor of the Allies," and Adenauer reciprocated by denouncing the Social Democrats as a threat to national existence.

In consequence, there could be no development of a political opposition in the sense of parliamentary democracy. The opposition either kept aloof and purely "against," or it sought to adapt itself, to be like the governing party, so as to win votes and come to power. There was no training the people in political thought by a frankly partisan struggle of minds. So a majority tended to cling to old habits, especially in prosperous times. The point of true politics, its function as the joint road to freedom in common existence—this did not even enter people's minds.

The point of a democratic opposition is to keep politics vital, by argument, by scrutiny, by a readiness to put divergent goals to the test in accepting governmental responsibility. It obliges the opposition to think and to conduct itself so that the factual objectives stated in its programs and political positions are worthy of credence. Though locked in a struggle for power, government and opposition must be friends on the common ground of one and the same national interest.

If we fail to recognize the opposition as a constructive power that the state cannot do without, we view it merely negatively, as an adversary, hostile to the state and thus in fact reprehensible. And an opposition without a program of its own—a program that has been thought through and affects the thinking of the people—seems merely a carbon copy of the ruling party. With the vanquished partisans the issues no longer carry political weight; they only care about winning a share in the government, no matter how.

Democratic freedom is gone when the opposition ceases to play its part as an indispensable factor in shaping the national will. For then the political struggle in the people's mind is over.

A parliamentary democracy that has not yet seen an orderly, legal transfer of power to the opposition is a doubtful democracy.

ALL-PARTY GOVERNMENT?

The failure to develop a constructive opposition, an interplay of government and opposition battling on a common ground, has its counterpart in the trend toward a "grand coalition," a government comprising all parties. Should this come to pass, our seeming democracy would vanish altogether in the authoritarian rule of a party oligarchy under the joint responsibility of all—in other words, under no responsibility at all. What would happen then is presumably not being planned. The consequences are not clear to the men who act upon such trends.

The parties would be left to themselves. They would share an interest in ruling. How they would rule, what they would do—all this would be shrouded in increasing secrecy. There would be no opposition, no curb on power. Inner struggles

would take the form of intrigues. Any truly political concept would be lacking, especially as the highest good would
not be the public welfare but the oligarchy's.

Elections would bring only trivial shifts in the relative
strength of the parties, the whole of which makes up the
oligarchy. And every four years the word would be: "The
people have spoken; the people can go home."

Patronage is a feature of all parliamentary democracies, and
there are no German statistics on its current extent in nonpolitical professions. Even today a physician, to become chief of a
city hospital, may prudently join the party of the city fathers.
But under an all-party government all nonpolitical jobs dependent on federal, state, or municipal funds would be distributed in proportion to party strength, as is now sometimes done
with religious denominations. An all-party government would
make it necessary for people in more and more trades to carry
party cards, no matter which. Their party would take care of
them; the man without a party card would suffer. The more
occupations came to depend on the state, the larger the rolls of
the ruling parties. Party membership would be the sole key to
private careers. Eventually every citizen would be a party
member.

THE OLIGARCHY OF PARTIES

Let me characterize the system of the oligarchy of parties.
To begin with, it preserves a number of parties against the
one-party system of dictatorship as well as against the free
party formation of a vital democracy. It establishes authoritarian rule by a minority of citizens who have appointed themselves to the promising job of politician. It is always by this
minority, this closed corporation, that the overwhelming majority of people are ruled.

A truly democratic will, the outgrowth of a state of republican liberty, would first seek out the best men, the most thoughtful, the men of judgment and vision—a minority, to be sure, but one that would be aristocratic in the literal sense of the word, not in the sense of birth and background. The very idea of democracy makes it simultaneously aristocratic. The influence of this self-regenerating aristocracy spreads throughout the environment, from the smallest circles to the whole population. The people only need to be left free, not to be enchained in parties, and not to have "the masses," a manipulated average, put in their place.

An oligarchy of parties appeals directly to the masses. It plays off the anonymity of large numbers against every individual. Essentially it has nothing to do with the majority, except at election time; and then the decision does not touch the firmly established, hidden solidarity of the party oligarchs, it affects only their relative share in their joint patrimony, the state. How they will conduct the election campaign, what instincts they will appeal to—these are the distinguishing marks of this kind of rule.

Democracy means self-education and information of the people. It means that people learn how to think, that they know what is going on, that they make judgments. Democracy constantly spurs the process of enlightenment.

Party oligarchy means contempt for the people. It means a tendency to keep things from the people, to prefer them stupid and ignorant of the oligarchy's goals—if it has any. Instead, the people can be offered stirring phrases, trite generalities, pompous moral pronouncements, and the like. They can be left permanently passive in their habits, their emotions, their untested accidental views.

An oligarchy of parties is insensitive to its joint lack of shame. It demands respect, rather, notably for its current top echelon of ministers, chancellors, presidents. After all, these men think, we are representatives of the people—how can we be shameless? Are we not hallowed by popular election? To insult us is to insult the people. Our jobs, they think, give us the power and the glory that is our due.

II

FROM THE OLIGARCHY TO A DICTATORSHIP

"Security"

Our strongest motive since the founding of the Federal Republic has probably been the desire for security. After the cataclysm we wanted nothing but a safe existence, to work and consume in peace, and to be secure in a stable state, under a stable government. Security became the greatest political good. Our latest election still produced such slogans as "Safety first," "Play it safe," and "No experiments." What about this security?

SECURITY IN THE CONSTITUTION

Our constitution was written in the light of what had occurred in 1933. The chance of a surprise totalitarian takeover was to be eliminated for all time. This kind of security became the first and foremost objective. Prevailing opinion placed the blame for the events of 1933 upon the institutions in effect at the time. To prevent a recurrence, one looked for institutions that would make it impossible.

The premise of this quest was that institutions, not men, had to be held responsible for the disaster. But it is the other way round, rather: the crucial fault lay with people. The best institutions cannot help if the men who use them will fail.

Thus the first flaw in our constitution is its orientation, the fact that its bearings were sought in the causes of Hitler's rise. The second flaw is the way of thinking of people who shared the responsibility for that rise and would now like to blame the institutions rather than themselves. And the third is the craving for security, the wish to prevent by laws what in politics can ultimately be prevented or caused by men only.

The analysis of any historic event is an endless endeavor, and so is the analysis of what led to 1933. The precedent conditions, a century of history, the special circumstances under which it really happened, the individuals who were temporarily able to push their way into key posts until their turn came to be removed—all this is an inexhaustible subject.

The treatment of that subject, whether in thought or in action, depends on a basic human attitude. History follows a necessary course, one man thinks; what happened had to happen. The other thinks: since men participate in setting it, the course of history is the one thing that is not necessary, for free acts as factors are due to something other than causality. In the objective view of causalities any concrete event proves unknowable as a whole, because the whole is infinite. We can see the given possibilities, the changing situations, the causalities, the coincidences—but we cannot see them to the end.

Let us apply this to the Nazi seizure of power. Demonstrable there is the rise of a state within the state; so is the energy of the Nazi leaders, who time and again dared to stake all on one throw of the dice; so is every situation in which they would best the politicians lacking in commitment, the ambiguous ones who seemed so shrewd in their calculations and were so blind to reality. Demonstrable, finally, is the inclination of broad masses (though not of a majority by any means, until March, 1933) to listen to Hitler and his promises in the vast misery of unemployment. But against all that stands the other view, in which I join. It did not have to happen, however stunned we may be to note all the factors that led to it, and the coming together of so many coincidences. The fact remains that, if men in positions of leadership had not opened the floodgates, the deluge would not have broken the dikes. It might have subsided; the first signs of its ebbing were already noticeable.

What happened was due, not to necessity, but to a combination of coincidences and to free human failures. The chances were there, of course, in the infinity of conditions. It was touch and go. But the seemingly most potent realities can dissolve all of a sudden. Those who had predicted Hitler's victory are most inclined, in retrospect, to regard it as necessary; those who had viewed it as impossible before it happened tend to think otherwise. But both sides, taking a historical view, might realize objectively that on the whole, while we can analyze ad infinitum and can differ in the weight we accord to the several causal factors, we can no more prove that an event was necessary than that it was impossible.

The concept of necessity has consequences for our basic view of life. Necessity justifies the victors: they only did what was due to be done anyway. It vindicates the vanquished: they could not succeed with the best of wills; necessity was against them. But a merely historic justification and a merely moral vindication are both fatal to an independent view of truth and to a sense of human responsibility.

We have to see the motives of the participants and the motives of the people, the impulses that freely arose and were freely affirmed or denied. Not until then do we see the root of the evil. Not until then can we grasp the meaning of the change that is required in our way of thinking.

WHOSE SECURITY?

Everyone wants a secure private existence and tends to judge politics, the sum of public events, by the measure of security that he expects it to afford him.

National security, then, means the security of all individuals, guaranteed by safeguarding the state as it is, the existing governmental structure, along with all the interests bound up with the state. The people demand security from foreign threats, and they demand security for themselves and their existence at home, in the domain of the oligarchy of parties. But the order of these securities is not the same for citizens and politicians. The oligarchy wants to secure itself. It equates itself with the country, and with the people. It protects itself with institutions and instruments ranging from the constitution down to the proposed emergency laws. Protection of the economy from disasters or recessions, protection from foreign powers—these, in fact, are put second. The security of the oligarchy of parties is identified with the security of the republic.

As a slogan "security" seems to express a matter of course. But it has many meanings. The cry for security mostly hides definite interests. An insistence on total security—which does not exist—has effects not produced by any meaningful search for security. It may have several consequences. One is that protection of the oligarchy of parties may finally stifle the West German people's political life. Another is that if we mean to safeguard the republic by making claims not recognized as legal by other countries, and if we proceed to call the nonfulfillment of these claims a threat to peace, we may jeopardize our security and turn ourselves into a potential cause of war. A nebulous view of the actual world situation leads to policies that add to insecurity while claiming to reduce it.

LIMITS OF SECURITY

In a democracy there is an elementary limit to security. We are secure as long as the majority prevails in case of discord. Resort to violence can be excluded only if the minority will always yield to the majority, reserving its right to change the majority by further persuasion. Without majority rule there is no functioning democracy.

But what if a majority vote abolishes democracy itself, the principle of majority rule? What if a majority bestows unlimited power on a minority, whether this is called "vanguard," elite, or "party"? What if the basic rights—which our constitution terms unchangeable by any vote, now or later—what if these rights are abolished by a majority? What if a free vote destroys freedom itself?

If we cannot communicate any more, if the republican way of mutual persuasion is abandoned, if things cease to evolve from power struggles carried on in legal forms, by reasoning together and against each other—if that happens, politics in the proper sense comes to an end. What then remains is either to give up (as the Weimar Republic did in the Enabling Act of 1933) or to resort to civil war.

Against a surrender of force to absolutism there can be no other protection than force. Should a minority give up when the majority proposes to subject it to irreversible force, to annihilate it? A people that would not prefer civil war to slavery in such a case is not a free people. Civil war alone can adequately settle such a crisis. If freedom is vanquished then, instead of being renounced in advance, a minority of the people has shown, at least, what it is and could be in its essence.

I repeat: The limit of any protection by institutions and laws lies in their dependence on the human beings who use them. In the emergency of threatened enslavement it is up to them, to those in positions of leadership, what they decide at the moment, on the instant, and what they will not do.

The limit of security lies where freedom itself is destroyed by false freedom, by a proposed legal abolition of legality. There is no absolute security in human affairs. The preservation of freedom takes freedom and involves risks. To want absolute security is to want unfreedom and political death.

Motivations on the Road to Dictatorship

Today, as far as we can see, there are no plans to set up a dictatorship. There is no purposeful leadership to that end, no organization, no Hitler. But there are coinciding forces, attitudes, and paths that may well take us in that direction.

THE STATE OF MIND: AUTHORITY AND SUBJECT

Centuries of authoritarian government have left us Germans with a residue of half-unconscious attitudes which remain strong to this day. There is respect for the government as such, no matter what kind, no matter how established. There is the need to worship the state in its representative politicians, as substitutes for king and emperor. There is the subject's awe of authority in all its forms, down to the lowliest clerk behind an office window; there is the readiness to obey blindly, the confidence that the government will do right. The subject thinks he need not bother his head about the government that looks after his welfare and his security in the world, the government that makes him proud to belong to a great nation entitled to make just and effective demands on other nations.

For a subject there is an aura about de facto rulers. However foolish they may act, their jobs hallow them, so to speak, and they themselves feel hallowed. They may take outrageous liberties, may sacrifice the public interest to personal feuds, may carry on intrigues and show the meanness of their spirit in political speeches. They still remain objects of reverence. In short, the way we feel toward our government is often still the way a subject feels; it is not the democratic attitude of a free citizen. A subject grumbles, to be sure, when grumbling is safe and will have no consequences, but he obeys, shows respect, and eschews action.

One symptom of this mentality is that our politicians want special legal protection from libel or slander for the federal president, the chancellor, the ministers—something like the old ban on lèse majesté. This is undemocratic. Every citizen enjoys the same protection from libel and slander, and no one, not even the president, needs any other. There is no aura of sanctity surrounding our rulers. On the contrary, it is desirable that they be exposed to relentless criticism. The man who dares accept such a position must know that high political and moral demands will be made of him, that he is exposing his every act to the glare of publicity and must stand up in it, that more will be asked of him than of others—not that he is entering a sheltered zone.

Should not a citizen also be free to express vehement disapproval in public when an Adenauer treats the presidency like some trivial bureaucratic function, wanting first to accept it and then turning it down, or when he backs the election campaign of his defense minister, Franz Josef Strauss, by asking, "What member will always tell parliament the unvarnished truth?" Or when Strauss is shown to have told untruths on the floor? Or when the minister in charge of the police speaks in the *Spiegel* case of "measures somewhat outside the bounds of legality" and declares in the wiretapping case that his officials cannot "run around with the constitution under their arms"?

At the start of the fight against *Der Spiegel* and its publisher, Rudolf Augstein, our federal chancellor exposed himself in the following parliamentary colloquy:

> We have an abyss of treason in the country. (Deputy Seuffert: Who says so?) I say so—(Seuffert: Are there legal proceedings pending about this, or not?)—because, ladies and gentlemen, when a sheet with a half million circulation will methodically and for profit commit treason—(Catcalls and hissing from the Social Democratic benches)—you see, gentlemen, then of course I felt it was my duty to get up here and to stand behind all those officials who have set with vigor about this extremely difficult and unpleasant task. . . . In this man Augstein, you see, there are two complexes. On the one hand he profits by treason, and that I find simply vile. And secondly, ladies and gentlemen, he also profits by his general agitation against the coalition parties . . .

These remarks evoked immediate contradiction and a detailed rebuttal from a Free Democrat, Deputy Doering, but in the end they were let pass. There was no public outcry. For a citizen wishing to have the state reflect his own dignity, Adenauer's utter insensitivity to the prompt and justified criticism was hard to take, but this too was allowed to pass.

Not one German took sufficient pride in his republic to lodge a protest that would have been to the point. No one wondered whether this was not "slanderous libel" and thus a reason to lift parliamentary immunity. No one considered whether the chancellor's conduct met the proper standards of a nation that wants to see itself in the man who governs it, and wants him to set an example of political morality. No one did, because the consequence would have been to look for another chancellor.

Here I may be permitted an interpolation. This book casts dark shadows on Konrad Adenauer, but that does not change the debt of gratitude we owe the man. We can never forget what we have experienced since 1945. It began with an event that passed our understanding: the American withdrawal from Thuringia. At the time, if we mentioned our fears to Americans, we heard: "You're still influenced by Goebbels' propaganda. The Russians are our friends. We can rely on their word." I was visited then by an Englishman who later rose to political prominence, a Platonist scholar who had once studied in Heidelberg: "We don't know what's really going on," he told me with a shrug, "and what the idea is." The subsequent change in this basic attitude was far from rapid. Once Adenauer got to talking with the Americans and other Western Allies, he tried with unflagging patience to open their eyes. The Americans' good will and actual interests worked in his favor, notably after the drift of things became clear. But it was Adenauer who in those days recognized the danger of all Germany going Communist in full view of the unsuspecting Americans, and it was he who drew the conclusion of unconditional adherence to the West. It was he who showed the Allies what might be done concretely in each situation, who got them step by step to make concessions helpful to both sides. Perhaps the Allies' own uncertainty made them seek his advice now and then. His German co-workers, in any case, found their sole support amid the prevailing helplessness in this man who was self-confident enough to dare it and always remained optimistic about the final outcome. He never gave up.

There is no telling whether it was really he who saved West Germany, at least, from Communism—whether things would have gone differently without him. To me it seemed so then, and I still think so. You could not read a Social Democratic platform in those days without cold shudders running down your spine, without the feeling that a united Germany recognized by Stalin might undergo something like the rape of Czechoslovakia. The Americans were still unaware of Russian cunning. The Russians, in Berlin, might have accomplished for the whole of Germany what the Americans would then have blindly accepted as an expression of the German will. Adenauer's memoirs provide some documentary evidence. I know of no other German politician who could have done what he did. Like others elsewhere, on a smaller scope, he served as proxy for all Germans in bearing the humiliations inflicted upon an impotent, conquered nation, an object of scorn and suspicion. He did it with a dignity that won him the enemies' respect, with prudence and with many ideas that impressed them, and with the pliancy of a counselor who sees what matters and will point it out in the events of each moment.

Adenauer has been likened to Bismarck. Quite apart from quality of mind, however, there is almost nothing comparable about the two men. Bismarck, with unique political skill and at a unique juncture of European diplomatic history, established the power of Prussia and Prussian-led Germany against a hostile world. Adenauer, with the aid of victors acting in their own self-interest, kept a powerless rump Germany in existence as part of the free West.

Yet the price was high. Adenauer thought exclusively in terms of foreign policy. Domestic politics interested him as a means of staying in power, in a position to carry out his foreign policy. This may be the one point of comparison with Bismarck. Both men unwittingly fostered tendencies that were bound to undermine the political ethics of the German people. Both helped time and again to break what spine there was in our national character. Domestically Adenauer had a baneful effect, as had Bismarck.

Eventually the aging Adenauer embarked on a foreign policy that seems to me to imperil Germany and the free West, whereas Bismarck's was for decades the grandiose peace policy which his successors proved unable to continue.

My doubts began in the fifties. In 1960 I expressed them

publicly. In this book they are no longer mere doubts. We do not yet have the free country we might have. Adenauer prevented it. Presumably he does not even understand what such a country of free men is like.

And are such politicians to be shielded from libel by special laws? In their case, the simple reporting of the facts is a libel which they have committed against themselves.

UNREADINESS FOR POLITICAL RESPONSIBILITY

One symptom of the state of our republic is that so very few people are ready and able to assume overall responsibility. Everyone is eager for some kind of backing, loath to undertake things he will be called to account for, afraid to be on his own, to be himself, to make decisions in earnest, and to answer for them. The accomplishments of business leaders and others fully deserving of their prestige lie in special fields, and they all expect to look up to someone above, to the government, to the statesman. They shrink from the higher task of assuming leadership and responsibility for the fate of the whole—in other words, from going into politics. And the vacuum is filled by men who boast of their ability to meet demands they may not even grasp, by men whose unshakable—but actually unjustified—self-confidence moves all those helpless subjects to put them upon a pedestal with the right to do as they please.

Whether or not they admit it, what citizens who keep dodging or shifting their personal responsibility want is to obey. They are preparing the way first for authoritarian rule, and then for dictatorship.

PARALYSIS OF POLITICAL THOUGHT

The consequence is that political thinking is paralyzed among the governed as well as in the government. The rulers lapse into a politics of drift, of mere activity, of a flow of words that add up neither to speech nor to spoken action, of having to take what happens to them, without learning from it. They fail to act because they only seem to have goals, because their objectives are either not serious, not heartfelt, or else they are unrealistic. At home our government is reduced to the action and regulation of an administrative bureaucracy, but bureaucrats can neither master politics nor truly change it. Our rulers act by whatever legislation will pass both houses of the federal parliament and by appropriating funds for specific purposes—in fact, serving the interests that promise votes on election day or money for the party coffers. In foreign affairs this government is reduced to a policy of legal claims without real substance. Legalistic thinking makes up for political thinking. The will to power seeks illusive satisfaction. Lacking substantial principles, this type of foreign policy will substitute dogmatic statements such as the "Hallstein Doctrine" of not recognizing countries that recognize Communist East Germany. These are not policies; they are roadblocks to policy.

THE COMMUNIST PARTY BAN

Another symptom of progress toward authoritarianism is the anxiety to protect ourselves by outlawing parties hostile to the state. The ban on the West German Communist Party was proclaimed by the highest federal court; constitutionally it was a legitimate measure. But from a political point of view it was undemocratic. Politically, a free people wants all its forces to contend in the open, though only with weapons of the mind, not with physical weapons. What does not appear in daylight will dig underground, poisoning the body politic. In a test of minds the hostile force can be fought and may be conquered; it is only where it turns violent and organizes for violence that the state power should intervene.

THE DECLINE OF CHECKS AND BALANCES

Our opposition parties adjust. They fight to win a share of power, not to curb the government. Investigating committees are a rarity, and one cannot help feeling that they do more to uphold the oligarchy of parties than to uncover facts for the people. The Heye case proved that parliamentary control, as it is supposed to be exercised through the commissioner for the Bundeswehr, is not taken seriously. Today the only true check seems to come from intellectual freedom—a freedom that leaves government and parties unimpressed, is blithely dismissed on occasion, and cannot often be adequate, with information so difficult to obtain. We still have that kind of check. Its principal example is *Der Spiegel*, a magazine that knows how to get an astonishing amount of facts by painstaking effort. The remaining checks—not really checks at all—lie in departmental and jurisdictional rivalries.

SECRECY

There is increasing pressure for secrecy that impairs truthfulness and even the reliability of justice. The veil of secrecy removes every restraint on the growing will to power. Acts of arbitrary rule become more frequent. Intrigues against freedom gain in scope.

The Paetsch case is an example. An official in the very bureau charged with the protection of the constitution had disclosed facts about the palpably unconstitutional practice of wiretapping. Referring to cooperation with the Allies on mail and telephone censorship, his immediate superior had told him, "This is about the most secret thing we have in the bureau. . . . Actually we aren't allowed to do it." Paetsch was indicted. Although he had only done his job of bringing violations of the constitution to light, he was not praised but prosecuted. It would befit a democracy of free men to oblige every official to publicize unconstitutional practices that are not promptly discontinued, and to protect such officials from reprisal.

We keep reading about the refusal of agencies to furnish information. I mention only a news item I have before me as I write these lines: "The numerous crashes of a new Air Force plane, the Starfighter, are causing concern. The inspector general of the Air Force, while vigorously denying German press reports that twenty-two of these planes have crashed this year, refuses to make the actual figure public."

"MINIMALIZATION" OF CIVIL RIGHTS

The road to dictatorship is marked by a tendency to "minimalize civil rights"—a phrase coined by a Social Democrat, Deputy Arndt. These rights should not only be unassailable; they should apply without limitations and be enforced to the maximum extent. Instead, they are treated with indifference or violated.

DEVALUATION OF THE MIND

Another harbinger of dictatorship is the incipient depreciation of the free mind. The question today is whether a crippling of education, of research, of intellectual life at large has already set in, whether initiative is declining all over. A man's advancement nowadays depends not so much on his mental and moral qualifications as on his connections, on the most varied kinds of loyalties, and on specialized technical competence. We cry for personalities and do our best to hamper their emergence and effectiveness. Hence the debility, the sluggishness of a life whose vital energies will either go into mere toil or evaporate in a void of talk, of demands, of abuse, of tranquilization. Neither in the operations of our businesses nor in our passing, swiftly forgotten excitements is there a faith or an ethos. The resulting human masses are conditioned for a dictator; they are all but asking for him.

To cover up our devaluation of the mind we pretend to honor it under the name of "culture."

SOVEREIGNTY

With the rise of our republic to the level of the world's leading economic powers, and with the development of our Bundeswehr into the strongest of European armies, the desire for absolute sovereignty has grown apace. It flies in the face of the fact that the Western powers, whose troops stand on German soil to protect the Federal Republic, have reserved the right to intervene against attempted uprisings or coups.

This will to be sovereign seems absurd. The presence of American troops is our vital safeguard against the East. Without them we should have perished a long time ago. Were they not garrisoned in West Berlin, all of Berlin would long have been Russian-occupied.

But beyond this there looms another question. Have we come far enough to trust our own ability to protect ourselves from forces hostile to freedom, and from its possibly all but unnoticeable overthrow by means of "emergency legislation"? There are far too few reliable libertarians occupying key posts in Germany today, and what the rest say and do even now is terrifying. Besides, there are facts such as the large number of subscribers to the ultra-rightist *National- und Soldatenzeitung*. We must protect ourselves from ourselves as long as necessary. The most outspoken advocates of absolute sovereignty are the antilibertarians.

The only lasting safeguard against disaster lies in the combination of an educated, public-spirited citizenry with appropriate institutions. And the more resolute the reaction to any first step toward loss of liberty, the stronger is the safeguard.

ALL-PARTY GOVERNMENT

One road to dictatorship, via authoritarian rule, would be the formation of an all-party government, a "grand coalition." This would hand absolute power to the oligarchy of parties. There would no longer be an effective opposition, let alone a chance of overturning that power. It would hold sway in ostensibly legal forms, not subject to controls, with a veil of maximum secrecy drawn over the real actions, the actual events. All struggles would be internal, would remain state secrets, and would essentially be due to personal rivalries and waged by means of intrigue.

EMPIRE, WEIMAR REPUBLIC, AND FEDERAL REPUBLIC

Let us compare the Federal Republic with the Weimar Republic and the empire of Wilhelm II.

There was no serious contention against the governmental structure of the Kaiser's Reich, however fondly Social Democrats and liberals might wish for parliamentary democracy under a constitutional monarch. Political thinkers such as Max Weber perceived the fatal weakness of an empire whose policy-makers were appointed officials rather than statesmen with the gift of leadership—for leaders emerge only from political struggle, which was nonexistent. Weber deplored the frightening superiority of Western statesmen over the German bureaucrats. The "system" was to blame.

The Weimar Republic did not command respect. The Reichswehr and a large part of the people were hostile to it, longing for a different state, for an undemocratic Reich or for the imperial monarchy. The body politic was crippled by internal tension, by the opposition of forces within itself. Germans looked upon this state as a symbol of their defeat in 1918. They could take no pride in it; they despised it. And the democratic forces produced neither impressive figures nor an enthusiasm for freedom and its responsibilities. They showed that they merely represented various interests; their petty disputes were over trifles; they displayed neither dignity nor political morality. All this led to Nazi rule.

The Federal Republic is virtually without domestic enemies. The Nazi remnants have no practical significance; an overwhelming majority finds Hitler easy to repudiate, notably since they would like to saddle him with the whole blame for troubles which in fact they brought upon themselves. But this state as such is a carrier of tendencies that make it an authoritarian structure. No monarch rules it, nor is one desired, but the state is turning itself into an authoritarian state with subjects whose spirit vividly recalls the days of the Kaiser. The very threat which in the Weimar Republic came from antistate forces in search of revolutionary change lies now in the state itself. It is not menaced by countermovements. No opposition transforms it. It transforms itself, vaguely pursuing the very aims that were pursued in those days: authority, authoritarian state, dictatorship.

"PATRIOT PARTY" VS. "LIBERTY PARTY"

There is another way to put this comparison of the three Germanys.

In World War I two parties may be said to have arisen, a "patriot party" and a "liberty party." The patriot party won, blocked every path to a negotiated peace—which it denounced as "quitting"—and brought about the great defeat.

The Weimar Republic was an attempt to found a new state in the spirit of the liberty party. But the spirit of the patriot party grew into outright hostility to the state and worked toward the Nazism of Hitler.

In the Federal Republic the patriot party is winning an all but unnoticeable victory by transforming the state.

What lies ahead on the road to dictatorship can still be prevented; but if the projected emergency laws should pass they will some day provide the means to accomplish it. There is a parallel to Hitler's realization that in Germany his only way to power—to the power which, once gained, allowed him to abolish all legality—was legality itself. With the help of the emergency laws, the new dictatorship would do the same.

A cleavage rends the German people's way of thinking, a rift that had existed long before it became so frighteningly plain in World War I. In this rift no German can help taking sides. We can be for political freedom or we can be for the unpolitical brutality of stubborn, unbridled self-will, for the refusal to think, to listen to reason, which hides behind a supposedly "patriotic" absolute power drive. If a man equivocates about this either-or, if he thinks it can be compromised, if he will not risk a civil war to keep the worst from happening, he has in fact made his unwitting and unwilling obeisance to the unpolitical, unthinking "patriot party."

The inhumane, illiberal power-seeker's strength lies in his fanaticism, in the "magic of extremism," as Nietzsche called it, in the tendency to bet all on one card and to be irresponsibly carried away by mass moods. It lies in a certainty of victory, in oversimplification, in breathless motion for motion's sake, in the lack of reflection and deliberation, in the method of blackmail, in the instinct for the jugular, and in hatred of everything liberal, humane, and free, of everything that makes us truly human.

The liberal's weakness is to trust the course of events, to expect reason to prevail, to wait and see, to keep looking for compromises even where compromise has become impossible. It lies in hesitation and delayed action, in a reluctance to commit one's total energies until compelled by the moment, until an overpowering desire for freedom sets in—if it is not too late. The liberal lacks constant enthusiasm for the political and personal liberty that is never secure. His daily freedom has come to be a habit; no longer quite conscious of it, he is tempted to grow passive, forget that the free are responsible for their freedom, and settle down to a comfortable enjoyment of existing, supposedly lasting liberties. The sense of danger flags. The ceaseless threat from violent power-seekers is not perceived any more.

Where this happens, where an area of freedom has been staked out and the perils are forgotten, that area will be filled with irresponsible criticism. Such critics negate for the sake of negation; lacking a sense of freedom, they apply ad hoc standards picked at random. Their criticism springs from personal ambition rather than from a will to improve free government. They are prepared to use force to come to power, as we have seen literati do in revolutionary times. Theirs is no mere adventurousness but a blind urge to be active so as to turn into something other than they are. Political freedom and personal liberalism make these people feel forsaken and empty. They long to fill the vacuum.

In part, such developments are the fault of democracy. A democratic citizenry tends to betray itself because it fails to grasp the meaning of republican liberty, because it shrinks from sacrifice and fears to risk its all for freedom, and for freedom only. Hence the triumph of those who want everything or nothing, who want it fanatically and are not afraid to die.

The Proposed Emergency Laws

The emergency legislation project is by far the most important domestic issue we face in the years ahead. It may create an instrument which at some fateful moment will make it possible for a dictatorship to be set up, for the constitution to be abolished, for an irreversible state of political unfreedom to be imposed, all in the same action. Moreover, it may cause the gravest threats to peace and may plunge Germany into a new, final holocaust that would mean annihilation.

THE PLANS AND THEIR TREATMENT

I cannot deal here with the plans for emergency legislation, with the proposed amendments to prevent abuse, with the years of conferences, with the government initiatives and the acquiescence of the opposition. The plans and the objections to them are known; the risks have been discussed; the crucial objections were raised first, I think, by Prime Minister Zinn of Hesse. Amazingly, however, the public at large remains unaware of the risks. They have been emphasized in print, but the press rarely touches upon them. Not even great newspapers take them seriously.

Purely negative criticism tends to be dismissed as fruitless, and indeed, the emergency laws adopted thus far seem to pose no threat as yet. The civilian call-up for air defense service is limited and the experience of the Hamburg flood disaster has shown the usefulness of certain laws for such invariably local emergencies.

The matter grows dubious when a Red menace is put forth as the case to prepare against. This menace did exist once, after 1945. Our protection against it lay with the Western Allies. Today the threat is a mirage.

One would expect our people to cry out in horror at the possible loss of their liberties and opportunities, at the chance that politicians with their heads turned by sheer bustle may unwittingly join the thugs in fashioning a noose for freedom's neck. Nobody will have the right to say he could not or did not know the consequences.

The government and the parties, however, are talking more or less in secret. Nothing whatever is being done to assure public discussion of the vast problems and perils. They are treated as if they were technical matters for experts.

I cannot report on all this. But I should like to point out some motivations from the realm of political ethics that play a part here, and some of the deceptions by which we are taken in.

EXTERNAL EMERGENCY

We distinguish between external and internal emergencies.

An external emergency exists in case of war. The idea is to pass laws that will make it possible in such a case to control the labor and the movements of the populace, and thus to assure its food supply and the orderly, uniform execution of whatever steps may be required. To this end it is deemed necessary to suspend such constitutional rights as the right to strike, freedom of the press, and freedom of speech.

The guiding notions date from wars of the past. They could have some justification only in the improbable case that a local European war should break out, as in Korea or Vietnam, and be waged without nuclear weapons—although a nuclear power threatened with defeat would surely use those weapons. But if, as can be expected, a European war were to turn at once into a world war, we run out of comparable situations. In the nuclear age war is total mutual destruction. There are in fact no measures against the emergency of such a war. This emergency must not occur. The consequence is that one must do absolutely everything to save the peace, and nothing that might lead to war. The only countermeasure to an external emergency is a sincere and unconditional peace policy (on which more later). For all the protest marches it has not yet sunk into the minds of our people, of our politicians, of our military men, what it means that war can and should no longer be the "last resort," the "continuation of diplomacy by other means"—and what the consequences are. At least the realization is still ineffective.

Emergency legislation for such a war will spur false hopes that even in that case we might not be beyond help. Such soothing will weaken the impulse to do everything to keep the situation from occurring. The words "No more war" apply today in a sense they never had before.

The new conditions have completely changed the point of the old military emergency measures. They would no longer save the fatherland or the people's homes or the people. What they would do for the moment—though only for a short time—is to permit a small number of politicians and officers to save themselves.

One of the plans for an external emergency envisions the construction of civilian bomb shelters. We find information on this point in an article by a leading physicist, C. F. von Weizsäcker, entitled "The Illusion of Security" (*Die Zeit*, December 25, 1964). If we can expect peace, he writes, shelters are superfluous; if an enemy wants to destroy Germany and the Germans—which Russia has the means to do—any protective measures are futile, and thus equally superfluous. It is only in the large range of contingencies between these extremes that we can discuss protective measures. But their value depends on the "war picture"—on the objectives of the belligerents at a particular time and on the changes in these objectives, above all on their escalation. The possible situations that would have to be considered are very numerous. They have not all been thought through by any means, and the usefulness of shelters, shelter materials, and so on, for the many possible special cases has not been clearly demonstrated by any means. Von Weizsäcker rejects the government-proposed program of increased protection (at a cost of $30 billion). One thing alone strikes him as definitely useful: an educational campaign to prepare people for sensible behavior in the face of war threats and incipient combat activities. "This preparation," he writes, "must be without any 'harmless coloring,' for today the truth about the possible course of hostilities cannot be concealed, and to detect any such coloring will make the public suspicious in peacetime and more prone to panic in case of war. The democratic system in which we profess to believe rests on the conviction that people can take the truth."

How an American optimist imagines civilian protection was recently shown by Edward Teller, the "father of the hydrogen bomb," in his book *Legacy of Hiroshima*.

The experts tell us that populations cannot be effectively protected from nuclear attack. What can be done, at enormous expense, is to build shelters for a very limited number. One such effective shelter, we hear, is the command post of the French *force de frappe* at Taverny, the site of its curious—because for practical purposes plainly senseless—war games.

We ask: What chosen few shall thus—how long?—be spared? The emergency laws give the people into the hands of that small group. The people themselves are in fact left to perish.

It is another form of the control which the military exercised over people and politics in 1914. Recurring now, it would have a more radical import, for today we are no longer dealing with war as conceived in past times. We are dealing with actions and events as they would happen now, in an age when man is undergoing a transformation that will either give him new, unpredictable capacities or bring about his doom.

We can no longer justify demands based on traditional military concepts. They express the egotism of a profession essentially still unadjusted to the new situation, the new tasks. The turn it must now take is not at all clear as yet. (More on this in the chapter on the Bundeswehr.)

The military must be radically stripped of control over

policy, of final decisions on the overall plans they have drawn up for military operations. It is the statesman's job to view the situation as a whole. This should have been done earlier; the precedence granted the military was one reason why World War I came about, and why we lost it. It is symbolic that when French troops mutinied then, Clemenceau went to the front in mufti and subdued the uprising; our Chancellor von Bethmann-Hollweg appeared in uniform even in the Reichstag, making speeches while the generals took action and set our course.

Do we want emergency laws to make a popular uprising against war impossible? Do we want a terroristic control mechanism to exclude the chance that people might resist everywhere?

Such a revolt would be magnificent, and it is possible. When there was talk of a plan to lay nuclear land mines on our eastern frontier—it was denied, but the denials were not given credence—we heard that peasants and police in the border zone were of one mind: "If the mines are laid," they agreed, "we'll dig them right out again." A rational people's hearts and minds can defy the irresponsibility of government and military. The police can rise against the government, the soldiers against the generals.

We have one great example. On October 28, 1918, with the war definitely lost, the 80,000-man German navy was picked to "save the nation's honor" by a "decisive battle." The combat alert signal was flashed on the high seas. What happened? The stokers doused the fires in the boilers, forcing the ships to return to port. The lunacy of an absolute militarism had rightly cost the officers their authority. Safely ashore, they wanted to regain it, and six hundred sailors were put under arrest. This second act of lunacy set off the so-called revolution which swiftly spread throughout Germany. The example shows how reason can prevail by disobedience. At some future moment of lunacy, acts like those are to be hoped for on both sides of the nations whipped into war. However unlikely, the chance must not be excluded.

If the worst happens, do we wish to entrust our future—or non-future, rather—to the military machine and a civilian government that does its bidding?

Do we wish our unthinking minds to be filled in advance with concepts and laws and ideas so wholly inadequate to the new realities that they will doom us finally and completely?

Would we not rather keep our freedom of movement if this extremity should befall us despite all political peace efforts? If we must die, do we not want to be free to die as we wish?

The enforcement of the projected emergency laws in case of war would turn the people into a flock of sheep driven to slaughter, led by the last politicians of the nationalist, absolutist brand. Such men, as power-mad as they are stupid, have a sense of compulsion in the disasters they have brought about, a sense of having no alternative. Actually directionless, taking orders from whichever source, they terrorize and are terrorized.

Should the catastrophe have one consequence for the mighty and another for the little man? Or should they, still equally free as citizens and human beings, make each his own choice under the conditions of their doom?

All people have a right to make their own decisions, and when their fate in catastrophe is at stake, this right can no longer be delegated to an elected government—least of all if this government would put the whole population into a kind of military straitjacket.

In this situation of our time a people unwilling to go to war must have the right and the chance to revolt—by strikes, by disobedience, by resistance to all those powers which cannot save us but would have us lose our liberty along with our lives. Perhaps the people would rather surrender and live, even with consequences just like the ones they resisted. But they want the chance of salvation. This chance does not lie in suspending freedom in emergencies. It lies, before any emergency, in the policy of a government that does not threaten other countries and so acts that no other country need feel threatened. And in an emergency it lies in the possibility of joint disobedience by the armies and peoples that are being spurred against each other.

The times are past when an external emergency could be treated as a contingency to be coped with by real and effective means.

There is a basic military turn of mind whose frank and candid statement would be, in substance: "If the world goes down it should go down in order." Against panic, the natural human reaction, the military mind does not rely on individual strength, which it thinks nonexistent, but on faith in authority. If men die according to rules, holding prescribed illusions, they will be less afraid. Such military thinking means that man's own self must be pulverized between the millstones of external and internal terror. He must be denied the right to die his own death, to feel his horror and his calm, to meet his fate lucidly.

To terrorize people into making an orderly end serves only to increase its inhumanity. This kind of order lets a man evade the seriousness of the situation; it makes him unfree and keeps him from being himself. However rationalized, it is irrational and stupid. A people with a sense of dignity must rise in outrage against the men and the measures to be imposed upon it, and against the blind fools who will do such a thing and not see it.

Total militarization robs a people of its soul. As human beings we want to know our fate, to face it and to bear it, to die as befits our doom.

INTERNAL EMERGENCY

In the Federal Republic there can be no internal emergency that would require a suspension of constitutional rights. Our people are unarmed, and so are our party organizations. There are no private armies in the Nazi pattern, nor is there a state within the state. No outburst of popular violence can be a match for the police power so long as this is at the government's disposal. If it is not, we should blame the government's folly.

The internal emergency is a fiction created by men. They would use it either to shore up power positions—to aid employers, for instance, by removing the right to strike—or else to suppress the dissent needed to maintain a freedom constantly jeopardized by an irrational government that ignores legality and basic rights. The people cannot abide the force that such a government uses; so they must have means of self-defense, ways of resisting without military weapons.

This is why political strikes must be possible. It was a political strike that defeated the Kapp putsch, the German rightists' attempt at a coup d'état in 1921. The military stood aside then, partly refusing to obey the legal government—on the ground that "Germans do not fire upon Germans"—or actually aiding the coup, firing on Germans after all.

With the people's part in policy-making and control severely limited thus far by our constitution, they have a particular need of the rights left to them—above all, of the right to strike, which the constitution explicitly guarantees them.

A memorable case occurred in Göttingen. The parties failed to agree on a candidate for the state ministry of education. He had to have a party card, and as there obviously was no man of stature on their lists, the God-forsaken party chieftains picked an individual who happened to be disqualified from the position of administering schools and universities. It was an extreme case. In Göttingen the students went on strike, and even the professors, little inclined to acts of that sort, voiced a protest: to have such a man for your superior was simply too much. The parties bristled. This was illegal, they said. The government was the people's choice, their representative and sole agent in the appointment of ministers; no legal basis existed for any protest, and the professors' attempt to arrogate a right of protest to themselves had to be vigorously rejected. Yet the minister turned out to be so utterly unfit to run the university that the Göttingers received support from educated circles throughout Germany. The government parties could not help themselves; they had to drop their minister. They then appointed another party member, a good man personally but wholly lacking in the experience and the breadth of vision required to deal with the problems of a university. In any case, he soon resigned.

The people must be free to manifest their will and their resistance by direct action. The emergency laws would rob them of their remaining means of resistance—means that are legitimate but would then be no longer legal. Such laws are shackles. Instead of passing emergency laws we should develop legal means to give the people some active role during their four-year abdication between elections. This would remedy our actual, present emergency, which borders on nongovernment.

The proposed laws would protect our rulers, not our people. In fact, laws that provide for declaring an internal emergency, and for steps to combat it, are steps to protect an oligarchy of our parties, the powers of its government, and the powerful interests linked with it, however selfish and irrational.

The government and the oligarchy must not be protected from the people. They are not the only ones who stand for the people; the people have other elected representatives in labor unions and employer associations, in farmers' leagues and other organizations. Besides, the people also exist as such, without intermediaries—though they cannot act as such, except in moments of overwhelming unanimity and vital resolution.

If a government, on the ground of emergency laws, resorts

to violence against nonviolence, against masses which offer passive resistance only, political ethics will justify the use of force against the government even if the law does not. Such force would be futile, of course, unless police and soldiers, both recruited from the people, should side with the people against their demented leaders. The least hope for such a stand can be placed in our officers, whose traditional esprit de corps and hidebound professionalism leaves them insensitive to existential realities and solely attuned to orders and effective force.

In any case of internal emergency—if one uses this word for strikes and disorders—the government should ask itself what it has done wrong. As long as the people have not formed an army, acts of violence can be met by police action and punished without difficulty. But strikes, protest marches, speeches, writings, and expressions of outrage are the legal and legitimate replies when abuses of power or the lack of a mere minimum of justice create conditions which the people cannot counteract by way of elections to the Bundestag.

THE INEVITABILITY OF ABUSE

With emergency legislation supposed to be good in itself, there is talk of its possible abuse. The powers that be, we hear, might bring about a situation and then declare it an emergency so as to create the premise on which the new state structure would void constitutional rights, and thus the basic law itself. Although the possible concrete event cannot, of course, be anticipated in a theoretical construction, it is believed that sufficient guarantees against abuse might be built into the emergency laws. But there is no way to prevent an abuse of such laws, for their principle is to exclude controls. In the end the principle of total force reappears behind any restrictive clauses. Without this principle there are no dictatorial powers.

Experience tells us that whatever a government does under

the cloak of legality—even a legal abolition of legality itself, such as the 1933 Enabling Act—will be taken in stride by the Germans as long as they do not notice what is going on. We cannot expect prompt resistance to an abuse of the emergency laws. The powers they grant are too terrifying.

On the other hand, we can be sure that they will be abused if the politicians involved are not reliably libertarian and democratic in their political ethics, as regrettably few are today. The threat is still greater if power is wielded by men who see no need for veracity, who wink at illegality and take wheeling and dealing for politics, by men who will play false, who are not credible and thus not trustworthy. If we get an emergency law we must reckon with the possibility that such politicians may hold key positions. People will give in, then, and cease to resist. With violence on the march, fear prevents an isolated individual from futile, suicidal exposure. He acts like everyone else, or he keeps quiet. We saw it in 1933, in our neighbors and in ourselves. Once the moment comes it is too late.

Recent events teach us that an abuse is not merely possible but probable. Remembering that men like Strauss and Adenauer could put the prosecuting officials in the *Spiegel* case into a state of panic as if the republic were in danger, that the Minister of Justice was left in the dark, that things "somewhat outside the bounds of legality" took place at the time— remembering this, we are bound to ask what would have stopped those men from declaring an emergency and proceeding to act at their pleasure if the law had been in force. Those incidents must never be forgotten in our country. The crack then suffered by the Federal Republic has not yet been mended; the wound has not yet healed. All conferees about emergency legislation must bear these facts in mind. To prevent abuses we shall have to do without such laws.

Their advocates have pointed to the grandiose phenomenon of the elected dictator in the days of the Roman republic. That dictatorship was a blessing during war emergencies; the political strength of the early Roman statesmen—of the senators, who were described as an "assembly of kings"—was such as to keep the dictator from becoming a menace. Later, as the selflessness of patriotic Roman statesmen declined, the form of dictatorship was the road that led first to the civil wars and then to the militarily based monarchy of the empire and the loss of political freedom.

DISTRUST

Our state structure rests upon fear and distrust of the people, but the people in turn do not sufficiently or effectively show the distrust of parties, governments, and politicians which they ought to feel at this time. Once again the subject mentality seems to be asserting itself, trusting the government to do right. This is the responsibility and the guilt of every one of our people. It was our undoing before 1914, and before 1933.

The hidden disparity seems nonexistent because it is not expressed. No trust is placed in the people, but they on their part will only occasionally and ineffectually distrust the oligarchy. There is no reaction in principle, no will to exercise control. The subject grumbles but remains beholden to the authorities. Neither side admits to itself what it thinks. Asked about it, both will say the contrary, demanding trust as if trusting were the self-evident, decent, moral thing to do.

How far can one trust a state and its representatives while acts deserving of the most profound distrust are committed—even though they are forgotten amazingly fast?

TOWARD A MILITARY DICTATORSHIP

The emergency laws would become tools of a military dictatorship. The present global trend is toward such dictatorship wherever nations are neither totalitarian nor capable of democratic freedom. A pure type of military dictatorship does not exist; its one common trait is the vital role played by the army in seizing and maintaining domestic power.

De Gaulle too started out in this fashion. He came to power through the army in Algeria, giving it false pledges. The whole was predicated on the nonresistance of a parliamentary democracy whose party politicians were in disarray, corrupt, senselessly splintered, and politically obtuse for all their individual acumen—for at crucial moments the few men of impressive insight would succumb to partisan concerns, to narrow party viewpoints, to coincidences. Then, when de Gaulle had legalized his power, when he broke his pledges and pursued a sensible Algerian policy against the army, the army became his deadly enemy. But all it could do then—in the famous night when its paratroops were expected to seize Paris, oust de Gaulle, and take over, in the night when he and Debré delivered their unforgettable emergency speeches—was to throw a scare into de Gaulle. The origin of his regime makes it a legalized military dictatorship, capable now of maintaining itself for a while without resort to military power. It can do so chiefly because de Gaulle's rule is humane, leaves the public spirit free, and exerts the magnetism of a dignified, highly cultured, oratorically brilliant personality, the embodiment of a great Frenchman.

As republicans (in the Kantian sense) we are committed to political liberty and thus opposed to such military dictatorships as Franco's and Salazar's, although these, unlike the totalitarian ones, claim no right to rule beyond their borders, either militarily or ideologically. The totalitarians, whether Communists or Nazis, claim that to be human is to live their way. They aim at world conquest and propose to force this way of life upon all men. Nonconformists, in their view, are worthless and must be exterminated.

The military dictatorships in Asia, Latin America, and Africa are something else again. If nations have never known political freedom, if they do not know what it is and do not want it, they cannot know what to do with it when it is imposed, and thus supposedly bestowed, upon them. They will find their pattern of order in a military dictatorship, with a variety of reasons determining its origin and the form it will take.

It is almost a miracle that there can be anything else, for at some point force is always indispensable to keep a state in being. That this force may be reduced to a minimum and channeled into legal forms is the miracle, the exception due to the strength of a people's will to be free. Political freedom implies the individual freedom of the many; where it fails, democracy first turns into a restrictive government and then into a despotic one. But freedom must be reacquired over and over, by education and tradition, in practice and in risk.

The Federal Republic would produce its own peculiar and presumably indirect type of military dictatorship. This would probably mean the definitive consolidation of the oligarchy of parties, which the military, in exchange for the fulfillment of its every wish, would uphold in fact. The oligarchy would submit to strict discipline by elected officials, would promote a military way of life for all, and would preserve the rule of law in most private areas, though not where political action and free thought are concerned.

EMERGENCY LAWS AND CONSTITUTION

The proposed emergency legislation cannot be said to "supplement" our constitution. What it amounts to is an authorization to repeal the constitution's guarantee of basic rights. It would have to be passed as a constitutional amendment, by a two-thirds majority. And though this majority would not be

taking a step equivalent to political suicide like the 1933 Enabling Act, it would be passing a law apt to have the same
results some day.

LABOR VIEWS AND THEIR LIMITATIONS

The Social Democratic zeal for emergency laws with safeguards against abuse is said to have been cooled off by organized labor. In an interesting interview a prominent union leader
named Brenner took a strong stand against all such laws. He
recalled that after a speech of his in which he mentioned our
continuing class society and the increasing entanglement of
economic power blocs with the machinery of government, the
then interior minister Gerhard Schröder was asked why we
needed an emergency law: "Well," said Schröder, "with the
kind of speeches Brenner makes. . . ." And an industry representative named Paulssen, asked why management always
yielded to union demands, explained: "We have to, as long as
there is no emergency law. They've got us over a barrel, with
the labor market as it is."

But then Brenner went on: "If you pursue a consistently
peaceful policy—like Kennedy's, for example—you don't need
to keep people in constant fear of possible aggression." What
an error! The contrary is true; our policies and our lives today
have to be built on concern—not necessarily on pure fear, but
on a fear-borne, fear-transcending sense of mankind's fate. Fear
may be abused for legislation that will provide a false security,
or no security, but fear is needed to come to the right peace
policy. Casting out fear makes men thoughtless and blocks the
high road to peace. Government and business may abuse fear
so as to crush freedom; but Brenner abuses the urge to enjoy
life, the pursuit of empty consumption and production, so as to
win power by fooling the masses. He demeans the idea which
men have of themselves. He encourages dissimulation in the

face of actual global violence. We must heighten our fears by looking truthfully at the realities if we would find roads to peace and accept the renunciations it requires. One thing that will have to be renounced is the will to power, as frightfully apparent among labor leaders as among leaders of the state and the economy. Power is legitimate only if it serves the ends of reason. Nothing else can make it meaningful. In itself, power is evil.

COMPARISON WITH THE NAZI UPHEAVAL

A sense of approaching disaster is the dark background against which we feel we live today. What is in store for us? "There must be a change" to avert catastrophe. Let us compare the situation with that of the 1920's, before Hitler came to power.

In those days all went well for a while, despite war reparations. And yet, among malcontents and those who had lost caste an ideological brew was already astir, needing only the rise in the unemployment rate to lead to Hitler's ascent. The ideologies made a most heterogeneous mixture. Their impact, enhanced by the metaphysical patter of some writers, was emotional rather than rational; amid the confusion of irrationality they constituted something like a faith. The citizens of the Weimar Republic lacked a turn of mind that would have linked them and enabled them to resist. Even so, the situation then was no more hopeless than it is today.

The differences are great. In those days want and unemployment—now prosperity. A state within the state arising then, in party organizations and armed bands, neither of which exist currently. Then a bewildering unrest, with helpless governments swiftly succeeding each other; today, for all our noisy party struggles, a governmental stability that casts a pall over our politics and may survive even what would be pompously called a "constitutional crisis." In 1933 the upheaval benefited one organized totalitarian party and one leader; now it would buttress the rule of an oligarchy of parties. Then the politicians of the past were removed in large numbers; now the effect would be to entrench the present party representatives in their posts.

The revolutionary process also would be quite different. The 1933 upheaval occurred under the central direction of the Nazis. Today the change would begin almost unnoticeably, not according to plans laid by an organization, not even in line with any widespread feeling.

There would, however, be the same militarization of everybody's way of life. People would be either giving or obeying orders. Planning would be general and rationalistic, beginning with an ever-broadened peacetime draft for civil defense— which after initial reluctance would expand into a patriotic function of the universal paramilitary sense of life.

SUMMARY

Let me restate my points.

A meaningful discussion of the consequences of emergency laws will have to deal with the real threats we face in the possible future. If there is a way to meet these threats it can only be truthfulness on the part of peoples and of politicians.

The people cannot be protected from nuclear warfare. Any claim that they can be so protected is a tranquilizer, dangerous because it weakens a possible defense against war itself. What can be done is to save a small minority by building underground shelters at enormous cost to the whole tax-paying population. Faith in peace is another tranquilizer, whereas outright fear of war will cause paralysis. False tranquillity and sheer intimidation both will doom any defense against the evil.

The questions we must ask ourselves are these. If the worst

happens, should people meet their nuclear death in a vise of coercive laws which would then be enforceable only by terror, or should they die free, unduped, aware of what is happening? Should freedom be curtailed or jeopardized in peacetime if this will be of no real help in a cataclysm? Since in fact the military cannot save us, should it totally control us at the end, together with its ally, the oligarchy of parties? Should a kind of Noah's Ark provide its self-chosen inmates, the men in positions of political or military power, with a chance to survive underground, to make a new beginning?

War has become something entirely new, but the quest of security by emergency laws follows the old lines of military thinking. Those past realities do not exist any more. Let us not fool ourselves about the scope of the havoc that would first hit the civilian populace. It is out of proportion to anything there ever was.

There are two basic political attitudes. A politician will either fear and despise the people or he will seriously, not just in talking for public consumption, reckon with and think of and for the people. In other words, there are politicians who do not want freedom, who are suspicious of it, who distrust humanity and accordingly wish to subordinate it—to place it under men who are just as human but supposedly called to rule, whether as vicars of God or as experts on historic necessity or as the vanguard of the future. And there are politicians who want all men to be free, whose every act or measure or law depends upon whether or not it promotes human freedom.

The power-hungry can make a chain of the very intricacy of the institutions, competences, and jurisdictions that are supposed to prevent abuse of the emergency laws. What we sense in the drafts of those laws, besides the immoderate desire for security, is sometimes a positive lust in promoting the laws. The complexity of this authorization to wipe out man's basic rights at one stroke would put all means of oppression at the disposal of an unlimited self-will, pleasing those who give the orders as well as the ones who carry them out.

And the others believe that emergency laws would protect the state, and thus their freedom. Poor fools! The dialectical process that leads from safeguarding freedom to crushing it endangers our political existence. At first the population will not notice it. It will all be done "legally," as in 1933, by act of the proper democratic institution. The state of emergency is a self-perpetuating instrument, a means to turn the exception—as against the normalcy of freedom and democracy—into the permanent state of government. This is true even though the drafts of the laws refer to time limits.

Since all governments and parties work through men, and since power corrupts men, power must be restricted. Power breeds more power, more absolute power. It obscures judgment. It becomes evil unless it serves an idea that will give it meaning and a relative end. A protection that allows power to become absolute is no protection. It destroys precisely what it is supposed to protect.

If I envision our possible course—from the oligarchy of parties to an authoritarian state, from the authoritarian state to dictatorship, and from dictatorship to war—I do not mean to say that I predict it. By outlining the possibility I want to make thinking men do their best to avoid this course. No one can know concretely where it would lead. The possibilities are endless. The changes in the world situation are incalculable. There is no predicting the motives of other powers which affect our existence.

It seems certain to me that trends which may eventually cost us our freedom are strong in our present parties—and equally certain that these trends need not prevail. If we see them in time, if we clear-headedly do not want them, we can check them.

It is almost incomprehensible that what goes on remains

unnoticed by a majority of our politicians and our people, including, as in the years before 1933, a majority of those who are making it come to pass.

And why are our allies, the true democracies, willing to give up their rights of intervention in an emergency? The only conceivable explanation is a fundamental trust in the West German people's and politicians' ability to help themselves— the same unjustified trust that is now placed in so many nations. The democracies have forgotten what happened in 1933, even if they remember the later crimes of the Third Reich.

III

THE BACKGROUND

The Federal Republic of Germany exists by the will of the Western Allies, exactly as the "German Democratic Republic" in the former Eastern zone of occupation exists by the will of Soviet Russia. We did not win our freedom by our own action, consciously fighting and sacrificing to establish ourselves. We got it free, as a gift, having done no more to deserve it than the East Germans had done to deserve their contrary lot. Both states rest upon the will of others. We must not forget this origin if we would solve the task that remains—to become free on our own.

In our republic it was the will of the Allies that returned the old politicians to power, the men responsible for the fact that the Germans had bowed to Hitler. These politicians and their associates formed the government and characterized the nascent Federal Republic. They had not emerged from the people in the free play of a new political life; they were actually imposed upon us, confirmed by a vote that gave us no alternative.

Our constitution is a fine piece of work, meticulously framed by thinking politicians and political scientists. It contains the traditional basic ideas of parliamentary democracy, and it proclaims the basic rights of man as inalienable, not to be changed by future parliamentary majorities. The constitution shows the pressure exerted by the memories of the Nazi scourge. Drawn up with one eye on the conditions precedent to 1933, it faults an institution, the constitution of Weimar, and aims at the institutional prevention of a recurrence. Hence its basic impulse, the quest of security. Its dominant idea is distrust of the people. It lacks all feeling for the nature of great politics, for the uncertainty of freedom in the storms of history. For it is on risk, on truthfulness toward oneself, on moral responsibility that freedom thrives.

The constitution was neither debated nor adopted by the people. They did not know it, and they could not understand it. Its ratification was a parliamentary act.

THE TASK THEN AND NOW

In 1945 our political and moral task was to found a new state. We have not performed it to this day. Our republic was set up by Germans, to be sure, but on Allied orders. It was the Allies, not the German people, who authorized some Germans to do the job. A plebiscite of ignorant men held in political darkness is no authorization.

The task of 1945 still faces us. We can perform it only within the institutional framework in which our state now exists. What makes the task much harder than it was in 1945 is the weight of institutional realities that have since been consolidated and have opened political paths, both foreign and domestic, which may well ruin us. It was much easier to restore our material living conditions than to regain our freedom of thought and political will.

THE CONSTITUTION THEN AND NOW

When the basic law was debated, drafted, and adopted, the
men who did this highly meritorious work were in an altogether different frame of mind than the politicians now governing. Germany was helpless and destitute. The "economic
miracle" had not yet come to pass, and no one expected it.
Rearmament was out of the question. The motto, not only of
Allied demands but of German planning, was "Never again."
The military will had been snuffed out, as had the will to
power. But there was a firm resolve to fit ourselves into the
free Western world by adopting our own republican form of
government (republican in Kant's sense) and a pure political
ethics.

Today we are lucky to have this constitution, despite its
flaws, despite its distrust of the people and its consequent
extensive curbing of the people's role. For here the inalienable
basic rights are clearly stated. Here are the conditions that give
us a chance to develop our freedom. On this rock alone stands
our free federal state, as long as the rock stands. The constitution must be graven into the hearts of our citizens. It must
never be forgotten by our politicians. Government and
officialdom must be aware of it at each moment. We have no
other fixed point in our body politic. Tampering with basic
rights will plunge us into an anarchy of evils from which the
exit is the brute force of dictatorship.

It fosters the ominous present condition that basic rights are
not always taken seriously. Our people scarcely know their
constitution. They lack the feeling that its violation is the
worst of political crimes because it jeopardizes our political
existence. Freedom perishes when basic rights are slighted.
Where the constitution permits itself to be amended or supple-
mented, these steps must be approached with the utmost cau-

tion, with public discussion and popular participation, before the decision is made by a parliamentary two-thirds majority.

THE BASIC UNTRUTH

Untruths lie at the core of our political life when we forget the actual origin of our republic, our unsolved task, and our basic law; and without casting light on these untruths we cannot hope for an auspicious evolution. Today a touch of mendacity pervades our political existence, and thus our personal one.

Such fundamental untruths poison a state.

But in our state the lies go deeper. They confront us, so to speak, at every step. Perhaps they can all be grouped around a single one: that the Germans were never really Nazis. That an incomprehensible fate delivered them into the hands of a wicked criminal. That at bottom, though terror may have beclouded their thinking at times (which is only human), they always remained as decent, peace-loving, and truthful as they had been previously and are today.

THE VACUUM

There has been talk of a vacuum in our political consciousness. And indeed, we still have no heartfelt political goals, no sense of standing on self-made ground, no inspiring will to freedom. We have not even a sense of the constitutional rock without which things would turn anarchic or despotic. The populace takes violations of the basic rights in stride, failing to understand that these rights signify the premises of our human dignity and civic pride. Our people are not yet democratically minded. We have a parliamentary form of government and call it democracy, although in its present rut it obscures rather than stimulates a democratic spirit. It not only fails to appeal to the citizens' sense of responsibility; it cripples it. It will not let them become citizens in the full sense of the word.

Nor is there a national spirit to fill the vacuum. Where such a spirit is not lacking it is artificial, tied to the past of a German Reich that has been definitely lost and whose restoration is a vain desire. This spirit focuses on the demand for reunification whose only practical role is the prevention of peace with the East. It does not engender a forward-looking and constructive political activity of its own. It is a pointless, mischief-making emotional outlet.

[The vacuum shows in the uncertainty and insecurity of political feeling among our people and our politicians alike. [Our government displeases, and so does our parliament.[One feels not truly represented by either.]They are despised in secret, and by some writers in public. As ruling powers, on the other hand, they have the respect of the subject mentality, as in the days of the Kaiser. [This vacillation between forced pride and lack of confidence in ourselves and our state shows how insecure we are.]

[Attempts to create national holidays, to make men conscious of their common substance, have been futile.] The unsuccessful attempt on Hitler's life on July 20, 1944, an event whose political significance remained ambiguous, could no more be celebrated than the failure of the workers' uprising in East Berlin on June 17, 1953. Nor could the date of the proclamation of the constitution—a day that had passed almost unnoticed, without an echo in the minds of the people supposed to be "constituting" their freedom—be turned into a holiday. Once, years ago, the attempt was made in the schools of one of our states, and I was told that when the ministry issued directives for the speeches to be delivered by the principals, the one word that did not occur in the model oration was "freedom." The attempt foundered on the apathy of teachers and students.

[We still have neither roots nor an ideal in politics, no sense of where we come from or where we are going, and hardly a present concern other than with our private welfare, with the good life, and with security. There are ways to overcome the vacuum. The first is to eliminate any untruth from the core of our political consciousness. The second is to want freedom on the basis of the instances found in our history, when freedom existed but fell into decay. And the third way is to address ourselves to our tasks in the present world situation.]

THE FREE SPIRIT AS A THIRD FORCE

The writers of a nation say what is. Their truthfulness can mobilize a people's thinking. They can clarify the will to political freedom and make it more resolute. But their words will go with the wind unless they are heeded by the people, by the politicians, by the governments. How is that in our republic?

Five years ago I wrote on "Freedom and Reunification," after a television interview in which I broached the thesis that what counts is not reunification but the liberation of the Germans in the East. For their freedom, I said, we could give up reunification. Then I heard from a student who had gone to Bonn with a few others to get material for articles planned by their student paper. They saw a prominent figure in each of the three parties; I was told the names. "In our questions," the student wrote, "we had to keep referring to your essay. It will interest you that the three politicians independently said the same thing: 'One can argue about Jaspers' theses, but we must object when he broadcasts his private views over such mass media as television, whether on his own initiative or on that of a TV station.'"

It was a trifling matter, and yet, when I read it I realized something I had not thought of before. The instinct of these politicians, in all the parties of this oligarchy, is to react defensively against the influence of the independent spirit. They want a monopoly on influencing the opinions that are broadcast to the people. The independent spirit may exist. The press does not bother the politicians; its 100,000 or 300,000 circulation will reach only a relative few. Nor do books matter, for they will not be known to any alarming extent. But mass media! That is where the gentlemen become sensitive. There they alone want to speak. They concede the same right to the opposition parties, but together they would, if they could, bar everyone else from the mass media, every independent writer or scholar. They want these media to impress their political concepts upon the public as matters of course, and otherwise to carry matters of political indifference. They have not yet gained their objective; important critical and informative forces remain at work in German radio and television, and one finds other indications of the same mentality.

But the government was able to launch a parliamentary attack upon Rolf Hochhuth, author of *The Deputy*. The chancellor could call him a "mutt" and could talk generally of degenerate art, of boobs and bunglers among German writers who turn political. Political writers can be, and are, disqualified as uninformed troublemakers. Thus the free spirit is not even respected, let alone welcomed in its activity. And yet it is what animates public life and raises a nation's prestige in the world. Above all, it can determine the ethos and the insight of its people.

Wherever the individual citizen decides the questions of political morality, wherever men turn away from error, from illusion, from false impulses, the independent spirit works as a third force between government and people. It might even help to determine the thought of political parties, to lift it out of sluggishness. This third force is the creative and inventive factor, if only in ideas and conceptions. It is the democratic public forum, both the arena and the vehicle for exercising the citizens' power of judgment. It is what makes men liberal and rational.

[In Germany, thus far, the tendency of government and parties has been to hamstring this third force, this illuminant of thoughts and feelings. The tendency seems on the increase.]

To the German political writers who follow the paths of rational insight it makes sense to dig up facts, to strive unconditionally for truth, to take the very publicity of their thinking for a sign that freedom is possible. Without acting themselves, they expect to participate in the political thought of the people and of the politicians.

The people generally still lack a clear view of the real dangers. As yet there is no will to change course. As yet we see no effective action by public men banding together for the great task. Nor are writers all of a kind. [There are the merely indignant ones who today will say a good many things which need saying, but with a touch of literary gamesmanship that makes their statements unserious.]

I would like to take up only one of the realities in this field. The *Spiegel* affair and its consequences seem to me to mark a turning point in the course of the republic. The real target of the fight against the news magazine was the independent spirit. This was to be crushed by the lawless and mendacious official assault, the most dangerous blow one could strike at a publication. But *Der Spiegel* survived, and that it could win this victory shows that when things are carried too far you will still find realistic libertarian forces in the Federal Republic. [We still have a government of laws.]

The first result was the large-scale exposure of a threat to freedom of speech. Almost the entire press recognized this and brought it to public notice, though at times with some hesitancy. A kind of popular uprising against wrong ensued, a rarity in our country.

The second result was the unmasking of questionable types

among our politicians. A few prominent names disappeared. That others remained in office is a symptom of our condition.

Third, despite the supposed impotence of the spirit, the affair caused a minister's downfall. The trap was sprung by the Free Democratic Party, since it takes political power to effect such an overthrow; but *Der Spiegel* furnished the weapons.

The effects were not limited to the republic, however. *Der Spiegel* also seems changed. The attempt to extinguish it succeeded only in bringing out the best in the magazine. Publisher Augstein did not fail in the battle that was forced upon him by the narrow-minded governmental powers. His defense was temperate, even magnanimous, but uncompromising. He triumphed without swagger.

Der Spiegel does not act, except by disclosure and criticism. It may be the first publication to have grown into an independent power factor in the West German world. It informs about events one does not hear of otherwise. In disciplined interviews it presents the men of our time, their thoughts, their style of argument. It does not fear to contradict itself, for it keeps moving and does not claim to own the truth.

It would be unfitting to look to the men of *Der Spiegel*, to Augstein, perhaps, for a future role in active politics. It is something altogether different to point things out, to exercise and demand vigilance. *Der Spiegel* is consistent in its refusal to take positive stands. I used to reproach it on that ground; now I see its wisdom. It is intended for free men in a free country, for men who want instruction rather than leading strings.

Der Spiegel has come to be our great, critical, oppositionist paper, independent of outside financing, independent of advertisers. It is an essential factor in the education of our public for a sense of reality and for independence of judgment. It exists and will remain powerful, we may hope, so long as no emergency laws bring dictatorship and unfreedom over the Federal Republic.

PERSONNEL POLICY

[In part, the present state of our country is due to the choice of personalities for political leadership.] They probably are not the best.

When the republic was founded, the unincriminated—that half-million or so of Germans who had never wavered—did not, or could not, take command. Was it an insoluble task? A majority of our people was seriously incriminated, though in varying measure and in varying ways. Now we were to form a new state and repudiate the old one as criminal, but the people, for the time being, remained the same. The mass prevailed; the minority kept silent and inactive. For a time the others were glad to have individual figures from this minority represent the new Germany before the victors, serving, as it were, to shield the majority. The incriminated benefited by the tolerance of the unincriminated, whether it was due to magnanimity or to opportunism. The unincriminated in turn failed to realize how radical a change was needed. They played a cozy, comfortable kind of politics and held their high offices with the consent of the incriminated, being not truly serious about the liberal demands but content with rhetoric. They were wanted as long as the new state with the old mentality had not yet won independent power. Once it had that power, once it began to look less and less like a new state, they became superfluous.

But the half-million or so who had kept their heads clear throughout and remained unincriminated were subsequently sidetracked or forced to see their libertarian idea tacitly thwarted rather than put into practice.

For our political reconstruction it was initially decisive what manner of men would take office throughout the top echelon, and who would influence the personnel policies pursued thereafter. One fact cannot be denied, although statistical evidence is hard to come by: formerly prominent Nazis did return to activity and to power. They were not satisfied with honest work in private occupations. Instead, with their peculiar ruthlessness and unconcerned self-assurance, they made demands and then kept raising their demands. An unspoken solidarity prevailed among them, working against the unincriminated, the free men whose mere existence reproached them.

There is a factual, if unorganized, community of interests among all those who feel incriminated and somehow possibly vulnerable because of something they wish they could erase from their past. A special case, but one of vital importance, is the Bundeswehr, whose organizers and present commanders are officers who followed Hitler, served in his army, shared the spirit of that army, and rejected the attempted coup of July 20, 1944. We had no other officers. If we wanted an army, we had to use these men as experts. But it was similar with our judges, our professors, our police, and so on.

The continued activity of old Nazis is a basic inner flaw in our republic. All of them condemn Hitler; all of them deny having been real Nazis. In 1945 the Americans used to joke about the fact that not one Nazi could be found in all of Germany. How subdued they were then, how anxious to explain that they had been misused, how humble and cautious even as late as 1948! Since then, along with economic recovery and with the country's new standing in the world, they have become more and more self-confident as co-directors of a seemingly restored great power.

They found allies in the shilly shalliers, the ones who would straddle this crucial issue of our republic. These men failed to realize the need for change. What they heard of it they took for unrealistic prattle. They dodged the basic choice that would have to precede concrete decisions in the situation of our new body politic.

Adenauer set the fatal example. Personally unincriminated,

he used his authority to keep as his chief aide the co-author of the Nazi race laws and their official interpreter. That this man could continue in office after his exposure, that he could remain the chancellor's useful tool, recommended by competence and absolute dependence on Adenauer—this was a fact encouraging similar conduct.

[But our new state cannot thrive unless high-level collaboration with the Nazi state absolutely disqualifies a man from political, moral, intellectual participation today.]He may have collaborated with the Nazi state by joining in particular wrongful acts, perhaps in death sentences as a judge or prosecutor, or by the literary explanation and vindication of Nazi principles ranging from the race theory and the treatment of Jews to the interpretation of the thesis, "The Fuehrer's will is the supreme law."[These were not crimes within the meaning of the penal code; but they were acts that showed a man's character to be such as to bar him from positions of prominence in a new state built upon a sense of freedom.]The deNazification procedure turned out to be the wrong method. However incriminated, the deNazified received a paper that spared them any further interrogation or investigation. The piece of paper was regarded as proof. Even against better knowledge, a government agency could appoint an official, citing this paper and feeling relieved of personal responsibility.

The actual choice of the persons now in positions of leadership lies at the root of the obstacles to a free unfoldment of our state. Constructive impulses are paralyzed. Like mildew, a spirit alien and inimical to the task blights the new edifice. If this spirit is not resisted it may ultimately destroy everything.

"NATIONAL CHARACTER"

[One answer we get when we ask about the cause of our political ills is the assertion of an immutable German character.

We hear that our national character is unpolitical, that Germans are politically stupid, blind to realities, given to dreams and illusions, entangled in theories, apt to obey without thinking, good-natured and barbarian at the same time. Sometimes openly, more often secretly, the free world thinks of the Germans as incapable of political freedom and thus not really capable of being reliable allies of free nations either. The world shudders to think of a possible new outbreak of madness; it is afraid of Germany.

Germans too cite their immutable character, and when they do, all hope ceases. No arguments, no education, no doctrine, and no experience will help. Just as an individual may say, "That's the way I am"—thus justifying himself and perhaps demanding sympathy for his being born that way—so there are Germans who tell their people and themselves, perhaps: "That's the way we Germans are." The curious plausibility of national character pictures rests on the construction of factually demonstrable moods. But other facts refute these individual aspects. In any case, they never apply to the whole. National character is not a comprehensible determinant of political fate.

It might give us pause that Spinoza, whose grandiose political thoughts aimed at liberty, did make such national distinctions. He lived among the Dutch, counted himself one of them, and there knew the successful struggle for freedom; but to his mind there were nations incapable of political freedom, such as the Turks. In this view I cannot follow Spinoza. What may look like a nation's permanently lasting quality is the ever-provisional result of its historic evolution. It is true, therefore, that nations cannot suddenly turn democratic, that they cannot be politically free and liberally minded from one day to the next. Today a majority of the people on earth do not yet know what freedom is. It is folly to treat them as if they were free already.

But we Germans are part of the common Western tradition. One cannot say that the Germans know nothing of freedom because they have so signally betrayed it. We do indeed need to change back to ourselves, to our historic roots. We are not damned to the hell of unfreedom. We do not need as much time as must be given to Asian or African peoples. We can be told: Now!

Today it is undeniable that few Germans tend to be politically active in their republic, that no one likes to make sacrifices in effort or money or risk for political ends, that many still fail to realize that politics decides the fate of all. Lack of time is no excuse. Most people have free hours and are at a lor how to spend them. And a man without regular leisure timᵉ one who is his own boss or the boss of others, can still make his own free disposition of his energies.

No historical or psychological knowledge can answer the question of our national character. The answer is given in action, given anew every moment—today by the German people of the Federal Republic. Our hope is that our people will produce the kind of politicians they can rightly trust, the kind who think along the same lines as the people and whose thinking clarifies the popular will. When those appear, the people will have to recognize and to heed them. That is the proof of their political character. If true politicians find no following, if our people will not listen to reason, will not respond to rational arguments, we are on the road to ruin. Our true politicians may then be forgotten as if they had never existed, or else their failure, as a token of another possibility, may serve to honor their nation in the memory of men.

We can cite many facts that justify despair if we take them for signs of something final and recurrent. A recent article in *Der Stern*, for instance, indicated that the German electorate will vote for the "bourgeois" right under any circumstances, even after catastrophes. In 1912 the Social Democrats emerged for the first time as the strongest party, but their 110 deputies faced 287 rightists. The rightist war policy caused the catastrophe of 1918, but the 1919 election still pitted 187 Social Democrats against 236 rightists. In November, 1932, despite the intervening economic catastrophe, we elected 121 Social Democrats as against 167 rightists (adding the Communists to the left and the Nazis to the right, the proportion was 221:361). And in the first election after the catastrophe of 1945 we sent 131 Social Democrats into the Bundestag against 261 rightists (with the extremists added again, the proportion was 146:266). The author of the article calls himself "not convinced" that the Social Democratic vote might ever rise to 51 per cent. This cautious closing phrase does not exclude the possibility, however.

We rest our hopes upon the contrary forces that have been visible in our forebears for a thousand years. As long as these forces continue to be detectable, however slight their power at any moment, we cannot give them up for lost. Without this hope such political writings as mine would be senseless.

A definitive character and personal responsibility are mutually exclusive. The Germans are not "the way they are," any more than any other people; they are what they make of themselves by virtue of their innate freedom. This means that they are responsible for their government. It is unjust to lay the blame for all evils on politicians, parties, and governments. This government would not exist if the Germans resolved not to have it. It has been said that a people has the government it deserves. All Germans have to answer for the fact of Hitler's rule; the guilt is shared by every individual who did not do what he could to prevent that rule before it happened, and did not do what he could to sabotage it afterwards. It is no different today. We, the people, are responsible for the politicians even if we disapprove of them. Each of us must to the best of his ability say and do publicly whatever helps the chances of reform. We must not try to evade responsibility by saying that this is the way the Germans are. Germans should listen to their writers; they should test the writers' thoughts by thinking them through. For the only way to prepare the people themselves for reforming their government is to spread insight and judgment.

This is why writers and journalists have a special responsibility. We have the right to ask whether they are always truthful, reporting facts without reservations, or whether they compromise and play a politics of their own, as though they were men of the acting, governing kind. We may ask whether vital information is not too often submerged in a tide of trivia, whether crucial facts are reiterated, whether the reader is made to think or a pseudo-wisdom serves to shield him from uncomfortable facts and from reflection on the consequences.

Calling the whole German people politically immature and unripe for free parliamentary democracy would be utterly irresponsible. If it were true—a case that could never be proved—no course would be left but resignation; and the few who are presumptuous enough to think they know would have occasion to scorn the fools and bullies and God-forsaken political helmsmen, and to retire to their ivory towers until the general doom engulfed them too. But one who has experienced the responsibility of freedom will not give up so long as he sees others whose courage does not fail on similar paths.

I V

POSSIBLE DOMESTIC
POLICIES

We cannot offer a program to be drawn up as a whole and carried out without thinking. But we can show possible directions of a German policy whose objects would be freedom, peace, and German dignity. I begin with the domestic field.

THE BASIC DECISION

A critical examination of present conditions and current trends could make us desperate enough to give up hope. It is a frightening fact that so many Germans—the best, perhaps—will emigrate. In America the opportunities and perils of mankind are manifest in their full magnitude. There you stand amidst the tides of fate. There you will not find the spirit of authoritarian government, of authoritarian thinking; or the rules of hierarchic demeanor which at our universities, for instance, extend all the way into social affairs; or all those provincialisms which every citizen of the Federal Republic must fight lest they suffocate him. I would not dare advise any would-be German emigrant to go or not to go. It is enough to tell him the facts and the possible significance of his new path, what he will and will not be relinquishing, and to tell him that in any event he need not cease to be German. It is no betrayal to find the condition and the evolution of the Federal Republic unbearable. If the republic is not to lose its best elements, as happened more than once in German history, it will have to find the way of truth and moral stature in politics on a worldwide scale.

The bulk of Germans who stay must find other ways of criticism. To conclude that this state ought not to exist is the wrong way, a purely negative one in which the critic is satisfied with exposure for exposure's sake, with indignation and vilification, and does it with relish. It will become an end in itself, and thus evil. Since so much of it is factually correct it will tempt men to live irresponsibly and to be nothing.

What matters is the conscious basic decision. The republic exists. Its existence is our point of departure. If I regard it as entirely corrupt in principle, its existence as wrong, the consequence would be to prepare for a violent revolution that would destroy it. Such negation is serious only if it has a goal, that is to say, if a man knows what he would like to achieve by overthrowing the republic. I can see nothing of the kind today, nothing to suggest even the possibility of a violent upheaval. Thus any meaningful political thinking requires both an affirmation of the republic and a will to change it from within—in other words, to employ legal, legitimate, democratic means to effect revolutionary changes in the minds of the citizens, and subsequently in their state. I do not reject our state; I reject the course of its government.

I can see nothing but evil in violent revolution, especially in the only kind we have so far been threatened with—the revolution from above, the kind that put an end to the Weimar

Republic in 1933 and might easily happen again as a result of emergency legislation. We have never had a revolution from below. In Germany this is a fiction, a bugaboo employed to scare people who want quiet and the status quo, who fear for their lives and for their property. It makes them amenable to the revolution from above, or to the use of force from above. We saw it happen here after the Napoleonic wars, after 1848, and time and again since, even in 1918–19. But there can be no free state and no free citizenry without the possibility of a "legitimate" nonviolent revolution from below, whether by political strikes, by mass protests, by a majority's refusal to vote, or by some other kind of direct popular action.

The true revolution is a revolution in our way of thinking. It seeks to convince, not to compel. Our state itself is affirmed in this revolution; its compulsory powers are needed for the protection of the legal, legitimate forms of political change; but no compulsion is required for the revolutionary purpose. The attack is not aimed at the republic. It is aimed at the government, and launched in the name of the republic.

PREMISES OF CHANGE

We do not want our new republic to fade into a transient, superficial regulatory structure, a structure that lacks any power of political morality but will turn violently coercive as the government falsely identifies itself with the state. Such a state would have originated by mere accident and would remain accidental until extinguished by another accident.

The new state necessitates a change in our way of thinking. One of the gravest threats to it is the passivity of "subjects" who will be content with their existence as long as they prosper. They will be docile and will not feel responsible in the least for the course of political events. They will submit to restraints which are all but unnoticeable, at first, and take some time to be recognized as a prison from which there is no escape. There will always be intelligent, vital, brutal individuals and willing accomplices. The populace becomes their prey—in Nazism on the largest scale, but other forms produce other phenomena. When we give free rein to our imagination, so as to see in the present what may come out of it, the threatening contingency sometimes seems tangibly close.

Today we need, first, an insight into present realities, and second, an insight into our past. How could it happen? It was not some natural process, not a fictitious historic necessity; it was free Germans who caused the events of 1933. Hence the definite question: Where did we go astray? Wherein lies the failure, the ill will, the cowardice, the untruthfulness, the evil; in short, wherein lies the guilt? Who, not what, is guilty, and in what sense?

Next, we need the will to take the consequences. The insight results in demands that are not easily met. We do not make them clear to ourselves; we struggle against them; we reject them when they are mentioned; we talk of the taboos, and then we bow to them.

The new state followed on conditions that could provide no basis for the future—first on the total collapse of political morality since 1933, then on total military defeat and unconditional surrender, finally on economic ruin. Hence the vital problem of finding the new, the right basis.

Economically this has been found. It was amazing how swiftly the hard work of a skilled, capable labor force, the competence of management, and a free market could bring about prosperity. But the economic basis is uncertain and inadequate. Without an ethical forming power of its own it is brittle. With the economy flourishing, owing to a tremendous effort by employees and employers, everyone wants to work less and less, to earn more and more, to have more leisure, to consume more, to enjoy himself more. Our economy may cause its own collapse if it is not subject to life-supporting ethical impulses, first among employers, who exemplify the spirit of their enterprises, and then among labor.

The political basis exists as a chance, thus far, but not yet as a popular political mentality on which the state might rest. It is not yet visible in the leadership and educational activity of statesmen. There exists no basis in the political ethos of a common public spirit. Not from a material point of view, but from that of political morality the situation of 1945 continues.

Germans who see this picture are deeply concerned. They know that to step on dangerous ground that merely seems to have been restored from the past would invite a new catastrophe. If we return to a so-called political normalcy because "the postwar period is over"; if we ignore what is implicit in our situation, that in the framework of a state created from without we must now build our own small, self-made state that will be free from within; if we view Nazism as an exception that is now over and done with—if we do this we are trifling during an interval that will prove far more crucial for the coming disaster than all previous intervals were for the disasters that ensued. This "normalcy" is simply the normalcy of muddling through—of being aimless, unserious, and secretly helpless. The one alternative that can save us is not a supposed normalcy but a political rebirth.

I should like to examine the concrete steps that may help us in our future. But devising possibilities is easy; I cannot always claim to have hit upon the best solution.

The goal throughout is to involve the people directly in political life, whether by a share in thought and judgment or by opportunities for actual participation. For a democracy— and that, after all, is what we want to be—the first question will always concern the people. The people ought to know their institutions and to use them, and the institutions ought to be such as to give the greatest possible scope to popular activity. Education ought to bring the people to themselves, as individuals meeting on a common ground, and to develop their capacities to the utmost. Domestic policies are valuable to the extent that they serve the people, turning out informed, perceptive, courageous, rational individuals who take a conscious, active part in the course of events. But let us not fool ourselves: any broadening of the people's legal ways to know and to act will be instinctively rejected by the oligarchy, by the old-fashioned, patriarchal bent of our good-natured but stupid Philistines, and by the cynical opportunists who are shrewd, scheming, and contemptuous of human nature. That the people are learning to use the means at hand—this is what creates today the necessary resistance to the deadly menace of the oligarchy of parties.

Institutions

Institutions serve to regulate political life and to provide safeguards against chaos and despotism. If our politics is to be kept vital and responsible, we must dispense with the kind of safeguards that would stifle it. We need a maximum of publicity and a reduction of official secrecy. We must subject personnel policies to the standards of political ethics and stimulate spontaneous popular action wherever possible. Here are some suggestions.

PARLIAMENT AND PARTIES; SECRECY; TREASON; CONTROLS

First, we should abolish the "5 per cent clause" that limits our parliament to parties garnering an arbitrary minimum of the popular vote. We should abolish the "constructive vote of no confidence" that prevents a parliamentary majority from voting the federal chancellor out of office unless his successor has already been picked. We should end the financing of parties from public funds.

The point is to break through the oligarchy. There is no danger of a party chaos bringing on a new Hitler, but there is danger that the oligarchy of parties may lead to an authoritarian state, and this in turn to dictatorship. Clinging to fears of a nonexistent menace aggravates the real menace.

Second, since our constitution leaves cabinet choices to the chancellor, we should make it customary for him, in his discretion, to appoint eminent independents or even members of the opposition. The point: to bring the best men into the government, and again to break through the oligarchy.

Third, a free country needs a maximum of public disclosure. Nothing else permits a maximum of truth and veracity. There must be no essential and permanent secrets. A citizen cannot take part in political thinking unless he is reliably informed and trains his judgment in public discussion.

If people are to be free, secrecy about governmental and administrative activities must be held to a minimum. In our republic, on the other hand, the government and the bureaucracies, including those of parties, unions, associations, all strive for a maximum of secrecy.

No one doubts that secrecy may be required temporarily—while negotiations are in progress, for example, or when a change in monetary policy is planned, in military questions or at certain stages of a criminal investigation. But the approach is what counts. Do we want to limit secrecy as far as possible, or is it the other way around? Do we want to keep more and more things secret because this facilitates what we are doing, because it frees us from curbs on our illegalities and lies?

If secrecy is prescribed for anything, it is reprehensible to "leak" it privately, to break confidences, to feed rumors. Men in positions that require secrecy have to observe it or to give up their positions. But it would be splendid if the law allowed or even obliged all office-holders who are questioned by the press, or who become involved in public controversy, to disclose facts whose disclosure would be in the interest of political freedom. When I was teaching in Heidelberg I once proposed empowering professors to make public what they have learned in dealing with the government. I pointed out, among other things, that in parliamentary debate the government may divulge what it pleases, whereas the professor who wants to reply is bound to official secrecy.

The criminal law on treason and betrayal of state secrets must be absolutely clear, and the regulations governing the secrecy to be maintained by officials must be so phrased that only a minimum stays secret, and that the bounds of this minimum are clearly defined. If there is a will to make our political life public, ways will be found to force it into the open. Once we are convinced that secrecy itself is evil we shall think of regulations to restrict the secrecy we need.

Fourth, there should be more and stronger controls. The government should, in practice, be kept under parliamentary control by investigating committees with the right and the duty to go outside the parties and the legislature, to consult independent experts and respected private citizens of unimpeachable political morality. Their findings—facts, opinions, and recommendations—would have to be made public.

Parliament should be kept under control by the people, by the press, by individuals, and not by way of quadrennial elections only. There should be a right of popular petition for information on certain subjects.

Control over the parties should be exercised first by themselves, by means of internal democracy, and then by enforcing the present requirement for an annual public report on the sources of all funds. We need a law providing very high fines for the concealment of funds by a political party, and for any trick to avoid reporting funds actually received.

As for patronage, there should be checks on appointment procedures, on selections, on the viewpoints determining preference—all to the end of keeping choices from being based on partisan, religious, or geographical considerations rather than on quality. And the cases in which such considerations may indeed be meaningful and justifiable ought to be clearly explained.

Finally, in the area of free speech there should be stringent curbs on any reprisals against men who say what they think. An extraordinary reinforcement of every citizen's protection from violations of his constitutional rights would be an institution like the Swedish ombudsman. Efforts in this direction are now being made in our republic; they deserve the fullest support. One might think along the following lines.

We now have only a parliamentary commissioner for the Bundeswehr; the point would be to extend the same protection to all citizens instead of restricting it to soldiers. The ombudsman would have the right to review any administrative act, to inspect any file, to question officials up to the cabinet level, whenever he suspects a violation of constitutional rights. The decision whether or not to take up a case would be his alone. Every citizen would have the right to appeal to him.

The ombudsman would need a large staff. His staff would be paid by the state, but chosen by himself. He would have immunity: no charges due to his official acts could be brought against him once he is out of office. His immunity could be lifted only for offenses against the penal law, by a three-fourths majority of the Bundestag.

And where to find such a man? Our experience with commissioners for the armed forces has shown that he could be neither a partisan choice, nor a parliamentary choice, nor a governmental choice. The ombudsman would have to be directly chosen by and from the people, like the old people's tribune in the free Roman republic. Nothing else would give him an authority of his own and the capacity to exercise real control.

THE PRESIDENCY

The federal president, under our present constitution, has no rights and duties that are properly political. The chancellor alone makes policy; the president must not intervene in behalf of any one political view. There are two different basic concepts of the presidential office. In either case the president stands above the parties: he may be a political power factor, as the people's choice, or he may have no independent power because he has not been chosen by the people. The second concept was intended in our constitution. The political neutrality of the office now lends it a dignity of its own, and a holder of the presidential mandate who becomes embroiled in active politics would violate this dignity without gaining actual political power of any consequence. He would fall short in his office because, once involved in political strife, he would have forfeited the unassailable prestige of his neutrality. Such action, by a president serving under our constitution, would be a symptom of confusion, suggesting a lack of political judgment and discernment. He would be doing great harm to the republic. Along with the dignity of his office, the one calm and suprapartisan pole of the state would vanish, and no noteworthy and effective political power of its own—the kind that goes with a differently conceived presidency—could arise in its stead.

The president has to appoint the chancellor, the cabinet ministers, and some federal officials, but he is not supposed to express his own opinion of their political posture or technical proficiency. His nonpartisan dignity permits, however, and indeed requires him to judge the political probity of the candidates proposed to him. He can refuse to appoint an authenticated moral failure. He could and should refuse to sign a second cabinet appointment decree for a man who in this capacity has lied to the parliament, even if the parties decide to forget the matter. If attacked for his refusal, the president could make his reasons public. His role, one highly desirable for the republic, would be like the Roman censor's: he could see to it that the positions of democratic leadership go only to morally outstanding or at least unassailable persons. One would hardly dare, then, to suggest any who are disqualified. The president would have to be calmly objective in his moral judgments, and he himself ought to be elected only on the ground of such a judicial temperament.

SPONTANEOUS POPULAR ORGANIZATIONS

Thus far our parliamentary democracy is representative only as a matter of form. How can it become truly representative? Are there ways for the people to take a direct part, aside from the balloting on election day which currently leaves any thinking person at a complete loss?

Are there ways, for instance, to let the people participate in the nomination of candidates? Or is that possible only by way of the parties, which comprise a tiny fraction of the population? Do all citizens have to carry a party card?

All this depends on popular initiative. A man with a subject mentality expects everything from the state, or from a large partisan or special interest organization, whereas a free citizen wants to make his political weight felt by his own activity.

Singly, of course, he cannot be effective. He must promptly and principally form a group, establish an organization. We Germans do this in many fields, but rarely in politics.

One would wish for private initiative to produce organizations that are neither parties nor partisan but will publicly state their free judgment, the result of their political inquiries and appraisals, and upon request will advise the government, the legislators, and the parties. In the United States there is a "National Committee for an Effective Congress," an independent group of eminent individuals. It does not support any party, but before an election it scrutinizes the candidates of both parties and endorses the best, no matter to which party they belong. The committee's integrity has given it great prestige; its endorsements are admitted to carry weight. It receives ample funds from private sources, thanks to the goodwill of civic-minded Americans. An atmosphere of nonpartisan, factually convincing cooperation ensues. One knows how to speak in the tone which this requires, a tone not set by aggressive impulses or witticisms at an opponent's expense.

We cannot simply duplicate this sort of organization, because our constitution, our parties, our electoral processes are different, if for no other reason. The great difficulty in the Federal Republic is the very slight leaning toward organizations guided by no hidden interest other than concern for the general welfare, for a politics of free men. To us, such bodies appear unrealistic. We do not think they can work. We distrust them.

If any groups of the kind exist here (the "Neighborhood Movement" based on the teachings of Artur Mahraun, for instance, with its meritorious publication *Ruf und Echo*), one still seems to hear in their professed independence an undertone of a distinct *Weltanschauung*. I do not mean to disparage them. They are convincingly honest, well intentioned, materially disinterested. It is good that they exist. And yet, as a whole and as of now, they seem to me too doctrinaire to attain the freedom that is possible in the United States. They show that there can be such an initiative in our republic, but they show also how strongly we tend to fundamentally exclusive views, how we relish planning for the millennium, how little store we set by the personality. We can change, of course. It will depend upon the education of all our people.

I would suggest having regular meetings and discussions at

the local level. In Basel, the Swiss city where I live, all parties are based upon their district clubs, eight in number, each comprising one city district. They meet regularly and elect their presidents. The presidents and representatives of the district clubs make up the highest party authority, the central committee. There the opinions and resolutions of the district clubs count; there the candidates they propose for general elections are sifted before final nominations are made on the party's behalf. Top-level politicians appear in the district club where they began their careers. It is a grass-roots democracy, a party structure with its basis among the people rather than in the bureaucratic party machine.

The "neighborhoods" would not need to be made up of party members if there were a popular concern with political education, information, and discussion, and if the people at the regular meetings included potential leaders, individuals who inspire confidence by their proved judgment, knowledge, and demeanor.

But a show of political ability outside the parties, without partisan direction, would still leave a man powerless. Without the chance of power it would have no attraction. Hence, if the parties have not usurped the state and turned it into an oligarchy of their own, such nonpartisan undertakings would have to be given certain rights and opportunities by the state. Men who have proved themselves there ought to receive diplomas that would be considered in evaluations for political employment, might qualify for official positions, and so forth.

The primary elections of nominees for general elections are in our republic an exclusive preserve of the party machines, whereas in the United States popular participation is achieved by allowing every citizen to have himself registered by the state in the party of his choice. He need not participate in party activities; he need not pay party dues; but he has a voice and a vote in primary elections.

Education

What becomes of a people depends upon its education—in the home, in school, and in the course of individual self-education. Its fate lies in the type of teachers it turns out, in the respect it shows them, in the atmosphere that prevails, the standards that apply, the things that are taken for granted in its everyday life. I can cite only a few points of political significance.

"Educate our youth!" goes the cry. Politicians cultivate the young politically. They spend money for schools, large sums of it, yet not enough.

The teacher's task at every stage from grade school to the university is to put the world he has to communicate to his students into a stimulating, mentally absorbing, character-building order and form. Then the disciplined work will make sense to the students and will not be a mere burden. This basic achievement, as laid down in books and realized in the classroom, means more than all material knowledge. We have excellent technical textbooks for mathematics, for grammar, for the natural sciences. But the history books are dubious, and modern books that might serve an overall philosophical (that is to say, intellectual and moral) education are lacking entirely.

The crux is the spirit of teaching and education. It must be so concentrated on essentials that distraction will be overcome.

SCIENCE AND CULTURE

As we talk of educational needs and the promotion of science, we have to make a distinction. The scientific instruction that is now technically necessary throughout our lives is something apart from the education that can provide our lives with guidance and fulfillment.

The sciences are specialized and teach definite skills. They must have their indispensable place in every citizen's existence. This is what makes us skilled workmen. It is as specialists, as experts each in his own limited field, that men possess specific knowledge and the skills required by their daily tasks. Scientific progress is the premise of technological progress and the basis of a future economy. To acquire skills, people must first have the will to be part of mankind's great march, to help form and develop the realities that make up our existence, to cooperate in the incalculable extension of man's mastery of nature and his liberation from the burden of mere toil.

Culture, on the other hand, belongs to man as such. All men can have it, and today it can no longer be a class culture, only a popular culture. To acquire culture, a people must first have the pedagogically animated will to find in culture its own infinite common bond.

FREEDOM AND AUTHORITY

Education is not drill; it is help in coming freely to oneself. It appeals to the freedom of man, not to his anthropological nature. It is accomplished as a student freely makes its subject matter his own. As authoritarian education it will fail.

Thus the demands made even on small children must be addressed to their freedom, so they come to see by themselves and learn from insight rather than obedience. Let them be scornful of incompetent teachers. They will freely respect the ones they learn something from, and they will love and revere teachers who wield authority without asking for it, by mere strength of character. If the authoritarian spirit of a school is not resisted by the student, it will be almost irrevocably impressed upon his still pliant and malleable nature. Such students will later be able to live in unconscious obedience and defiance, but not in freedom.

INSTRUCTION AND STUDY

There is no getting around the rigid discipline of mental work and its enforcement against inclinations, pleasures, distractions. This discipline militates against the pseudo-freedom of license. The everyday activity of education requires incessant practice; otherwise it brings forth nothing but talk and deception. Nothing great can become visible and effective without such discipline. It is as necessary for culture as for the acquisition of specialized knowledge and skills.

SUBJECT MATTER

What makes us human is that we can feel reverent, that we can make products of the mind our own and have them permeate our conceptions, thoughts, and impulses. As we actively assimilate works of letters and art, the contents pass from the works into our souls. A Westerner should be at home in the Greco-Roman world and in the Bible. He need not even know the ancient languages nowadays, with good translations in inexpensive editions incomparably more accessible than ever. It is as though the simplicity and depth of greatness in antiquity were adding a new dimension to our life, showing us human nobility and setting standards. To know nothing of antiquity is to be unawakened, to remain barbarian. A man's whole life is marked by whatever contents of tradition he has absorbed in school, from early childhood on, without having to reflect upon them. Sins of omission committed against a child are hard to make up later.

HISTORY

As an educational factor history is indispensable. It makes us at home in our background, in the life of nations and of mankind. It enables us to understand what men have done, experienced, seen, and wrought. But this understanding can lead us astray, to wrong turns which may decisively affect our political thinking. We may come to think we understand the necessary course of things. The charm of Hegel, of Marx, of Spengler, and of a phraseology that is now almost universal lies in a delusive knowledge.

The demonstrable delusion is to mistake comprehensible connections for causal necessities. In fact, they are nothing but constructions of ideal types. They are evident in themselves, but how far reality conforms to them remains a question. What we can point out as historic causality is always particular, always manifold, and never a necessity of events as a whole. One tends to forget the role of coincidence in events that can be neither foreseen nor understood later; one will overlook the creative leaps in history and cease to marvel at the inexplicable things that have happened to man, and through man. The origin of symbolic, mystical, moral experiences, of concepts of divinity, of sacred norms which suddenly, as by some miracle, exist at the outset of civilizations five or six thousand years before Christ and instantly attain top rank—all this cannot be explained by any necessity, and it gives us hope for the future.

A concomitant of the belief in a knowable necessity is either passive fatalism—since we cannot change what has to come— or the fanatical activity of those who feel not only aware of, but as one with, the necessary course of things. To such men wishful dreams become realities; no fact can refute them; they will risk all, being sure to gain all by historic necessity.

Another peril is inherent in historic understanding: we may lose our sense of rank. In the nature of things, comprehensible history will either attract us or repel us. Various people will be variously affected; comprehension implies an existential judgment. We may, however, make the mistake of thinking that once something has been understood as "historic" it is thereby justified. Everything will seem entirely good, then, or neither good nor bad—*tout comprendre, c'est tout pardonner.*

"Grand designs," patterns of the history of mankind and of certain sequences, make sense at particular times, but they are drawn up in different forms, none of which can be the one that is valid. They do show us something, more or less, as we try for an overall view. Classic high points will move into the foreground of the educationally vital themes. The ethos of the examples gives us standards that are concretely infinite rather than generally doctrinal.

In history we see ourselves at a place in time, so to speak, wondering where we come from and where we may be going. We see ourselves entirely in the present: the more so, the clearer the past and the more inscrutable the future.

GERMAN HISTORY

Today, after a great, fateful caesura, we have to make a new start in approaching our own history. The bare facts have not changed, but the emphasis has. If we are honest in looking at ourselves and our political thinking, we see a new dividing line between the essential and the unessential parts of our history. A clear, new historic consciousness has become crucial. Above all, we need today a history of liberty in German lands, in the framework of the Western history we are a part of.

Our situation seems insoluble because the way we look at it as we experience it is untruthful. Its main requirement is that we be true to the facts of the most recent past, and able to judge it. The guilt was not Hitler's; it was that of the Germans who followed him. (Had Hitler been brought to trial, the court would not have denied his "faculty of free will," our German test of criminal responsibility; but he would have been granted "diminished responsibility" on the ground of psychiatric testimony about the organic illness that can be traced back to his twelfth year: encephalitis lethargica with ensuing Parkinson's disease. See Johann Rechtenwald, *Woran hat Adolf Hitler gelitten?* Munich & Basel, 1963.)

Today we face no Hitler and no Auschwitz, nor any similar threat, but Germans as a whole seem unregenerated from the way of thinking that allowed Hitler to rule. Now that we are a prospering society of producers and consumers, are we going to remain so satisfied with the moment, so blind to facts, so fanciful, so irresponsible, so mendacious? If so, we are asking for trouble quite unlike the one that Hitler caused us, and we shall feel no greater responsibility for it than a majority of Germans felt and are continuing to feel for the fact of Hitler's regime. To see our condition from the standpoint of political ethics, we must know history, the facts, and what is comprehensible about them. Any madness seems as possible today as ever. History illuminates the present not only by showing what was and will never recur, but by showing what was and is still with us.

POLITICAL EDUCATION

As children begin to mature they need education in political thinking. They must be put in touch with public affairs, with the realities of the body politic. To prepare them for the life of voting adults with a share in personal responsibility for public affairs, they should begin in school to exercise what is now known as the "students' share of responsibility." They should undertake common tasks, should meet, debate, confer, and make decisions about the things they encounter in school, the things that concern them.

Political education must never cease. Citizens need a maximum of information and participation in political activity. For the crucial part of political education is practice, which includes the joint performance of tasks on the smallest scale.

Political education takes a way of thinking that must be trained, a kind of knowledge that must be acquired. It does not thrive in talk and in distracting discussions, only in the discipline of continuous application. The way of thinking I mean is a weighing, testing one in the flow of arguments and counter-arguments. If my mind is open I can hear what my opponent thinks and can even help him present his thoughts consistently and strongly. I can put myself in his place. I can tentatively suspend my initial position. I have the patience to develop all possibilities to the fullest extent.

Three orientations are of primary importance in political thinking.

We must acknowledge the reality of force. The will to be nonviolent cannot abolish force; it is a hard reality and not to be talked out of existence. Wherever it seems to have vanished in peaceful, private situations, we forget that even this happy existence is somewhere based upon a force that has been applied, or is being applied, by others. The nonviolent are beneficiaries of such force. And even in peacefulness itself some kind of force may suddenly reassert itself. For political purposes force is not the norm, of course, but it is a limiting factor. The very believer in notions of absolute nonviolence will be so much the more violent some day.

Realities are difficult to determine exactly. In particular, we must distinguish how far they are given as inevitably extant, and how far they are changeable.

The true point of politics is the establishment, consolidation, and preservation of freedom in the form of a state. In this sense it aims at liberty for all. A free man feels free only if the rest are free; this is why in politics he will be democratic, liberal, and "partisan"—if one still wants to call it that—against brute force, against authoritarian, dictatorial, totalitarian trends. He knows there must be dominion, but he will not have men dominate their fellows otherwise than for a time, subject to controls, and at the people's bidding.

Force, reality, and freedom never coincide in lasting harmony. Politically things remain in flux. Political education trains us to think so that in this flux, feeling it, sharing it, without denying force and reality, we try as best we can to channel it so it will serve the true politics of freedom.

It is not enough to be carried away by great but vague ideas of truth and liberty. If they are not clearly thought through they make us stumble and stray. Political thinking takes knowledge. Political education means book learning as well.

The first thing to be taught in our republic is the constitution, the cornerstone of our existence as a free country, our only firm support, which must not be weakened.

Then the main works of political thought should be studied. Plato, Aristotle, Cicero, Machiavelli, Hobbes, Spinoza, Kant, Tocqueville, Max Weber—these are examples of the authors to choose from. What counts is thorough treatment, not the production of scatterbrained know-it-alls who can cite slogans and formulas without having thought about and understood them. Without knowledge and practice in the study of the great political thinkers our own political horizon remains narrow. To comprehend the vastness in the present world situation—something actually new that determines the fate of us all—we need the vastness of the political thought handed down to us by the few political thinkers.

Issues of the day ought to be dealt with. They alone are the contemporary, concrete, directly interesting, and exciting topics which book learning helps us grasp.

The speeches and acts of contemporary politicians also should be analyzed in political education. We must not shrink from showing the young what exists and what goes on. But what we should chiefly arouse in them is respect for the human being and for the rank of individuals—without idolatry, for even with the greatest we reserve the right to criticize and to perceive the limitations of all men.

Finally, political education should convey the experience and the insight that in case of conflict there must be a following. In the very smallest groups we see born leaders loved and recognized, and on a larger scale the fate of all hangs on the crucial decisions in which the leader's reliability, the followers' devotion, and the mutual loyalty of both must tell. In no other way can anything enduring, unifying, and continually creative come about.

Skeptical questions will be raised about this education. Where to find the educators? Are there any? What sort of community might furnish the locale? How to rouse an interest in politics among the young, among the indifferent?

Certainly our parties cannot provide a proper political education, for they would mostly influence it in a partisan and prejudicial sense. It is not party service but community service that makes for good education. It would have to be provided outside the parties, in an independent spirit, at schools and universities. Groupings set up on free initiative—mentioned above as possibilities—would be especially suitable fonts of such education.

The result must be an arena for the political thought of all citizens and a meeting ground of parties and ideologies as well. Educated political thinking is independent thinking. Parties should be organs of the people, devices to bring the best of the people into contention for the right to represent the whole; but political thinking as public education should occur on the common ground where all those who want freedom can meet before going on to partisan political activity. The party politician too should have learned to remain ultimately independent of his party, and he should keep learning it over and over. He can change parties. There must be no governing *Weltanschauung* other than the will to be rational, truthful, and factual.

V

THE BUNDESWEHR

The Bundeswehr is the Federal Republic's largest, most powerful, most solid instrument. Universal military service makes it an arm of the state which the citizen feels more intensely than any other. The sacrifices it demands cut deeper than taxpaying.

We cannot do without the Bundeswehr. We need it for the American alliance, which protects us so long as we participate in our protection. When Adenauer, contrary to all his previous statements, undertook to rearm and thereby to accept a relatively large measure of sovereignty, his decision seemed to me hard to bear but unavoidable, and so it seems to me still. The idea of neutralizing all of Germany without a German army was an illusion. Who would not wish to live in such a paradise of undisturbed well-being, secure in a guaranteed peace? The paradise might have lasted for a short while, perhaps, although in fact in the utmost insecurity. Any war between the other powers would have found us at their mercy. We need this army because even neutrality can be maintained only if it can be defended.

What the Bundeswehr is and should be is perhaps the most

vital question facing our republic, because its consequences are the most momentous. Nobody can say it has been solved, but neither does it seem possible now to draw up plans for a convincing solution. All we can do for the present is pose the problems and discuss them without reservation. They must not be swept under the rug or covered up with pseudosolutions drawn from a tradition that is no longer realistic. We must not be satisfied with the mere practical workings of a defense force that is vague about its tasks and goals and develops no spirit that would give it meaning and coherence.

The Bundeswehr is not a problem for itself alone, but for every citizen and for the country. The Heye case, which shed a moment's light on the situation, was widely resented and quickly forgotten. But the problem concerns us all. Every citizen of the republic should watch what is really going on, and make a judgment whether this is what he wants.

For the Bundeswehr will cast the nation's lot. It will be fatal if it embarks on a course of claiming precedence in politics and in the life of the people. Its weight is equally great in domestic and in foreign policy. At home it can lead the way to despotism and cost us our freedom. Abroad it can cause a war and cost us our existence. It cannot perform its great function unless a sense of the situation of modern weapons technology and global politics fits it into the great goals of Europe, of the West, of mankind, with a will to peace and freedom.

THE NEW CIRCUMSTANCES

The new soldier. Man, both as a civilian and as a soldier, finds himself today in an utterly new situation. The age of technology, of atom bombs, rockets, and space travel, has wrought a change in weapons that is qualitative, not merely quantitative. The soldier in the sense of past times is no more than a romantic relic like the World War I cavalryman riding senselessly to his death. The soldier of today is a technician. The idea of this soldier as a moral figure has not yet clearly emerged.

The pace of weapons development. Military technology is changing at a pace that may make yesterday's planning senseless. Aerial bombing has been replaced by ICBM's. The dropping of bombs from satellites in space seems imminent.

The development of atom bombs, of missiles, possibly of antimissile missiles, and of a global network of observation posts proceeds so fast that what small nations are producing and planning is obsolete by the time they reach their goals. In case of war their weapons would be useless. If France were to launch her atom bombs against Russia, they would probably fail to reach their targets, for Russia has means of defense; the one sure thing is that France would be laid waste in a matter of hours. America and Russia have attained a level that makes the rest fall farther and farther behind. Their resources do not allow them to catch up. In space the two are now competing alone; there is no one else yet who might follow suit. But it may well be in space that a world war will be decided, although all sides today forswear its military use.

By sheer power, by economic strength and technological superiority, the two superpowers can afford to keep the rest at a distance that is not only wide today but widening. The Big Two vie with each other, advancing as they do; we others cannot even think of entering the competition. In a general war we would be doomed anyway, unless one of the superpowers could protect us with an assist from our own small military force.

Global strategy. The superpowers think in terms of boundless space, for their military technology works worldwide. Strategy becomes world strategy. And the world strategic situation is in constant flux. New possibilities will arise, above all, once China has to be reckoned with as a nuclear power. But even earlier, with only the two superpowers planning for every contingency and thinking it through, the changes in weaponry will not leave much unaffected.

All the rest, all the small nations, receive consideration as pawns in this great game of global strategy. The parts they play, or the extent to which some may keep out for the time being, will be determined by the superpowers.

World war and local wars. At present, in any case, there is no immediate threat of a world war. Today it would break out only if America and Russia fought each other. This is possible, but it grows less and less likely. The "balance of terror" has become monstrous enough to convince both powers that war would be suicidal. The astounding fact is that the development of weapons technology seems to have made such a war all but impossible. By now, if there were no nuclear bombs, Europe would most likely be at war again. The situation has led to a tacit accord between two superpowers, which for the present, at least, seem to remain deadly enemies at peace.

Local wars are a different matter. They are not only possible but a fact. They are being waged all the time, with all horrors, with greater cruelty than ever, but without nuclear bombs.

For the Bundeswehr the crucial question is this: Can there be a local European war, or would such a war—whether started by Russia attacking the West or by the Federal Republic attacking the East, to regain the old German frontiers—instantly become a world war? Must our army be ready for a local European war or only for a world war, or for both?

What role can our army play in a world war? Lacking all the premises of active participation in global strategy, it could act only within the framework set by the American and Russian strategists. It would have its role assigned to it by the superpowers, not by its own planners.

In the work being done at the Pentagon, in this weighing and thinking through of almost infinite possibilities and ever-changing situations, in the constant new starts that must be made there—in all of this, presumably, the Bundeswehr has no hand.

It must ask itself certain questions. What is it doing that is superfluous, useless, in vain? And what does it fail to do that should be done? The layman trying to inform himself from reports cannot get a clear picture, aside from the simple basic facts. He is not told what concepts prevail in the Bundeswehr, if any. Is its thinking realistic and meaningful? Is it aware of its own situation in a global perspective? We hope so, but we cannot tell. A citizen of the republic has not a trace of an inkling. Everything is secret, even what need not be secret.

The necessity for peace. Part of the new situation is a need which in this form has never yet existed in human history. War used to be regarded as inevitable, eternal peace as a dream to be realized only in an infinitely distant future, however much a suffering world might yearn for it. But today a nuclear world war is something that has brought all thinking people to the same conviction: in the nuclear age we must no longer think of war as inevitable.

Men used to say: *Si vis pacem, para bellum*—if you want peace, prepare for war. And they were not just being insincere. Today the advice is sincere but almost impossible to take. Arm to the teeth, it says; use all your strength to increase your skill in the use of destructive weapons—but be as grimly determined never to employ them. How can your entire life turn about a machine that is never used in earnest? Yet today this is what military preparation means.

Professional soldiers are understandably inclined to put their professional skills to the test of battle. What the present situation demands of them seems absurd. And yet, it is now vital for the Bundeswehr to stamp out every rudiment of that mentality likely to breed actions leading to war. If a general says, for example, "We will regain our eastern borders, peacefully or by war," he should be promptly and ignominiously cashiered.

CHANGES REQUIRED IN THE MILITARY MIND

Obedience as a way of life. An army necessarily demands authority and gets it by compelling men to obey while on duty. This authority lies in the nature of the case; limited to its specific purpose and not intruding on the living patterns of the personality, it is not intolerable. What must be vigorously countered, however, is the tendency to carry this obedience and this authority beyond the realm of military duty. Off duty, soldiers must be free to wear civilian clothes. There must be no control of private conduct, of ideology, of opinion; no questions must be asked about religious or party affiliation. Every soldier is a free citizen who submits to the exigencies of military service within the bounds of such service. An extension of the duty of obedience to off-duty areas is tantamount to a militarization of life.

Universal military service is a massing of the people's energies in the hands of the military power, for military purposes. It must not degenerate into a tendency to view the people as matériel for tasks of force, and to transform them by militarism.

For once the military power becomes absolute we lose the very thing whose protection is the only point of force—our existence as free men who will defend their freedom.

Freedom in the army. There can be no freedom unless it is given scope and weight in the army itself. Obedience has its clearly delimited sphere. Off duty, and in every material respect, officers and men are equals. They will comport themselves as equals if they are a community of free men.

Freedom erodes if men need the power of command to feel sure of themselves. Count Baudissin's term for the principle of a free soldiery—"citizens in uniform"—has found general acceptance; but there are those who view this as a passing phase with which they must put up for the time being. Men of this bent will not take the matter seriously, and since it is meant most seriously they become liars.

No privileged officer class. Building the military establishment is the professional task of officers and noncommissioned officers. Their profession is a necessary one. But the tendency to consider it a privileged one, to rank it above others, to invest it with special glamour, is unjustified. We hear complaints that the profession is losing caste. They come from people who miss the old social prestige of the Kaiser's officer corps and even of Hitler's—a prestige with ruinous moral and political consequences. Officers were singled out then as a special class above all others. Uniforms were worn in preference to civilian attire, and a civilian would feel that nothing but a commission in the reserves established his worth as a man. We have done with that; it ought not to recur in a free democracy.

The officers once had the glamour of death-defying men. The civilian populace was not in danger of life, and so that made a qualitative difference. Today the reverse is true: the relatively safest berth in wartime is the officer's. The civilians' share in the casualty rate has risen; it has become many times that of the uniformed force. Since World War II it has kept rising. Civilians are no longer safe.

THE DANGERS

There are three main threats to the army's spirit and ethos, to its "inner command," to use a currently popular term.

"*Tradition.*" The Bundeswehr had to be built with the same officers who served obediently in Hitler's army and overwhelmingly opposed the attempt on his life in July, 1944. There were no other experts. Without them there could have been no army. How powerful their kind of spirit has remained to this day became apparent when a columnist, Countess Marion Dönhoff of *Die Zeit*, wrote an illuminating article on General Guderian. The furor of dissent from her factually incontrovertible characterization of the eminent tank specialist as Hitler's man was frightening.

It remains an open question whether the Bundeswehr with its actually new and altogether different tasks is still pervaded by the old conceptions, by the old manners of consorting in command and obedience, by the old spirit that inhibits performance of the new tasks as much as it offends a citizen's dignity. This basic question was raised by Admiral Heye and remained unanswered.

It is the question of tradition. We are right to seek models and ideals. But there is no getting around it: our first need is a radical break with the immediate tradition, the one dating from the time of Hitler's army.

The German army's moral decay under Hitler, after feeble attempts to resist, has been demonstrated by too many published facts to need further expounding. To cite just one representative scene from Baron Kunrat von Hammerstein's book *Spähtrupp:* on January 25, 1944, Himmler and Goebbels summoned 250 Wehrmacht generals and admirals from every front to a meeting in Poznan. Himmler informed them that all Jews including women and children were to be liquidated. The "final solution," says Hammerstein, was thus "disclosed to the largest wartime gathering of German generals. Some had known since 1942 about mass shootings to exterminate Jewish population groups in the occupied Eastern areas. At Poznan General Reinicke walked to the platform after Himmler's

speech, to express humble thanks. . . . Back in the audience
one general made a quick count: five were not applauding."

Based on his personal knowledge—a knowledge which by
now might well be general—Hammerstein addressed a letter to
the editor of the *Frankfurter Allgemeine Zeitung*, against an
article which this leading German daily had carried in December, 1955.

To me [he wrote] the danger that the new troops might make us
oblivious and give rise to a Hitler myth seems relatively slight. But
you seem bent on creating a myth of the field marshals of the Third
Reich, for the benefit of those now building our new army. This
effort cannot be opposed strongly enough, in my view. Your question how a war would have gone without Hitler's interference is
misplaced, for there would not have been any war in the first place.
No democratic German government would have begun one as
Hitler did. Most of the army commanders of World War II were
quite familiar with its point of departure, and sooner or later they
also became convinced that the war could never be won. Despite
this conviction, the generals—aside from the few well-known
exceptions—conducted operations in accord with Hitler's will,
though at times, perhaps, with some reluctance. Aside from the
praiseworthy exceptions, the marshals ventured no attempt to save
their country by removing Hitler. Few of the army commanders
of World War II were Nazis; but their comprehensive knowledge
of the situation, their training, and their position imposed on them
a heavy responsibility for the nation's fate—a responsibility they
cannot unload on Hitler's shoulders. This is why the invention of
a field marshals' myth is the last thing one should do to help build
up our new defense forces.

Let me repeat: a tradition derived from the Nazi era will
corrupt the spirit of the Bundeswehr in its roots. We need a
radical break with this tradition, and the establishment of a
new one. Its premise would be the negation of the spirit of the
generals and officers of the Nazi era. The new tradition might
look for moral support to the spirit of the great soldiers in the
German past, of Gneisenau, Scharnhorst, Clausewitz, the elder

Moltke. In fact, the Bundeswehr is engaged in something quite new, something which so far is only a challenge: giving the army a new meaning under the conditions imposed by weapons technology, global strategy, and the political situation in our world.

Some misunderstandings are due to the obfuscating equation of generals and soldiers. An officer will issue or transmit commands while a soldier does not command at all: he obeys. I remember men I used to know—a classical scholar, for example, who had been a reserve officer in World War I. Reporting for duty when Hitler brought about his war, this man said he did not wish to dodge the universal German fate but requested reactivation as a common soldier, not as an officer. In this Germany he felt unable to give orders or to pass them on. "It does not really matter who wins," said another; "what matters is whether I risk my own life to bring food and water to a comrade." If generals contend that they were used, this is simply not so. They had the responsibility of command and went along. Only enlisted men can truly claim to have had their valor misused to the point of self-sacrifice on behalf of a mirage. Although this is true of many Germans who were so minded, it is precisely not true of the generals. The truly heroic, numerically insignificant exceptions died on the gallows—put there by the actions, or by the inaction, of fellow generals—but the rest were cowards, in a deeper sense, devoid of exemplary qualities, and not entitled to a place in tradition. To realize this is essential to the change on which a new tradition may be founded.

What powerful forces from Nazi days block this realization was shown by General Heusinger's belated order of the day calling for recognition of the sublime sacrifice made by the plotters of July, 1944. If these resistance fighters are now finally to be the basis of our military self-assurance, the cornerstone on which to build, the men who use them for their own exculpation are liars. The bulk of our generals continued to disown those real heroes even after the catastrophe of 1945.

False pride. The tremendous development of the Bundeswehr has had an effect that threatens peace. Many Germans are dissatisfied with the position of the Federal Republic. They feel that its production and its army both are ultimately serving foreign interests. It hurts their pride to see how it is treated. They want to regain the status of an independent world power. They want more than their present insignificance. But where is the increment to come from? It could only be derived from integration into the world history of freedom, from participation in the development and self-preservation of this freedom which is still threatened by the vast numerical superiority of the unfree world. Today it is this integration alone, no longer a political concern about national sovereignty, that can clarify the meaning and purpose of our republic. Nothing else will let the Bundeswehr consider itself on a worthy level. The cry for another increment, for more of something else, would give us less—by plunging us into dictatorship, into militarism, into claims of absolute sovereignty, into Luciferian adventures and eventual perdition.

The mere will to use military and economic strength as means of pressure jeopardizes the peace. It does so even if one does not want war, as before 1914.

Today, as long as it remains integrated into NATO, the Bundeswehr cannot act independently even if it wished to. But already we hear voices toying with the idea of withdrawal, of making our army as independent as de Gaulle is making the French one. Should this occur, the Bundeswehr would be a menace to the Federal Republic and to the world.

Shielding the government from the people. Today, as in the days of warring German states, the Bundeswehr as a West German army poses a joint threat with the East German army.

It must never be used against Germans, not even as a means of pressure.

Moreover, to stay free we do need revolutionary movements and changes—not false, violent revolutions and coups d'état but revolution by all legal means up to the political general strike. Coups are a police problem. If the police force itself joins a popular movement and can no longer be relied upon, the misdirected governmental authority has lost its rights. The vital point, then, is that the army must never be used to "restore order." Once the Bundeswehr goes into action against the German people—or against popular movements which the police, in case of violence, cannot or will not handle—freedom is lost. Where is the guarantee that this will not happen? It would take a free, democratic spirit in the ranks and a corresponding spirit in the army as a whole to start mutinies against attempts to use it at home, against Germans.

We have by no means come far enough on the way to change to feel reestablished and sure of ourselves, of our reason, and of our will to be free. We are still largely the persons we were before 1933 and under Hitler. We still have to reckon with our worst potentialities. We still face ourselves with a fear derived from experience; we dread the forces in our people that produced such horrors. The horrors may recur, not identically but in other ways. Once again the republic's government and army might succumb to delusions. We have seen it all—the faith that defies facts and evidence, the total irrationality, the magic of extremism, the intoxication men plunge into, blindly, ready to make any sacrifice; and the consummate technical rationalism, coupled with an equally consummate political fatuousness that calculates victories, thinks in purely military terms without purpose or goal, and coerces the people—who are indeed quite happily coerced for a while and then go on obeying to the point of self-destruction.

We know the arguments. One must not hurt a nation's pride,

we hear; one must not damp the people's spirit by constant reiteration of the evil facts. No, I say—the full truth must sink in; there must be no remnant of equivocation and self-deception if we are to regain our proper pride and discount the false pride. Lying, we hear, is all right for the common good, because otherwise you cannot get along in reality. No, I say—nothing but unreserved truthfulness can make us change and prevent our definitive destruction.

KNOWING THE PROBLEMS AND CONTROLLING THE BUNDESWEHR

Our military planners may well feel baffled by the incalculable possibilities and by the ever-changing complexity of the problems. They cannot answer the questions of overall planning. They cannot tell what to do or not to do, what will make sense and when, what is needless or futile, and what may suddenly have vast importance.

None of the problems are solved. First, in any case, we must be fully aware of them. Every soldier, every officer, every citizen ought to ask questions about the world situation and what it means for the Bundeswehr. What the individual knows will determine his actions, and those will help to decide about war and peace. His duty is to do everything in his power to promote peace, and to counteract everything that might foment war.

This brings us to the question of the spirit of the Bundeswehr, of its "inner command." The duties of our new army are not limited to the performance of the military tasks assigned to it by the government. Beyond that, it has to put the democratic and liberal spirit which the republic requires into daily practice, aided by instruction and education.

The army, it has been said, can only be as good as the democracy it serves. Considering the realities of our democracy this is a sad judgment. In actuality, it takes army and government together to provide the requirements of the citizens' internal and external freedom. Only together can they find the ways to the change that leads to restoration.

The army's task requires that its "inner command" be entrusted to political personalities who see its purpose in safeguarding freedom in the world, not in serving limited interests of national power.

The control of the Bundeswehr, of generals and officer corps, is one of the gravest parliamentary responsibilities. That our legislators, so far, have not realized this gravity—that in a concrete instance, in the Heye case, they have actually failed—is one of the worst symptoms of our political condition.

There was a storm of protest recently when someone called the Bundeswehr a "state within the state." And indeed, at the moment it is not. But it is true that its potential power outweighs everything else, that it is lavishly financed by the state, and that this army is our only public organization not inwardly shaking. Without the fear that it might turn into a state within the state, without a look at German history in which this happened over and over, we are not going to keep it from happening again.

VI

FOREIGN POLICY

There have been men on earth for half a million years, perhaps for millions. A mere six thousand years of high mental creativity and continuous tradition make up the conscious history on which we stand. Today, after half a century of slow preparation, we are in a technological metamorphosis that proceeds at breakneck speed and affects all mankind. We grow dizzy thinking about the facts and seeing ourselves in this cataract of history. Where are we going? To our doom, or to a new human condition that is still invisible and remains to be created, to evolutions we are not yet dreaming of? We do not know. The future is veiled. All things are weirdly unstable.

History shows that men have hardly ever thought responsibly and realistically about mankind as a whole, not even about preserving a specific civilization. Every political and cultural dominion won thus far has been gambled away.

World War I is the latest example. Europe had been ruling the globe; as a result of that war she not only lost her world mastery but found herself menaced by two giant superpowers, the United States and Russia. She could no longer preserve herself alone, by her own means. Today we can ask a question that was vainly pondered by some individuals before 1914: What would have happened if Germany and Britain had teamed up? Germany would have had to do without a navy, and Britain would have had to admit Germany's factual hegemony on the continent. Germany's booming world trade would have made incalculable strides under the protection of British rule of the seas, but despite her bases and colonies Germany would have been unable to challenge Britain by force. She would have played second fiddle in this alliance. Yet the two between them might have upheld European rule and perhaps educated the colonial peoples for an increasing equality in times to come, as the British had begun to do in India. It was a utopian idea, but the failure to take it up led to the consequences we see now.

History does not encourage us. What it seems to show is irrationality, coincidence, and total failure.

We may conclude that we are going to do the same all over, except that this time our follies and passions will doom us all—not just one dominion, not just one civilization, but all of civilization and human existence itself.

But in us lies a will to realize the incalculable possibilities of this worldly life of ours, a desire for more than living that can be fulfilled only by living, a will that this world should go on. And this will makes us say that humanity must not destroy itself. This may be a human limitation. Jesus and some old Hindu philosophers cared nothing for the world's existence or else they viewed it as agony, as chaff, as evil. They were at home elsewhere. They did not need a world, or a life in the world. We are quite different, as shown by the way we live in fact. Men who speak in such terms today seem to deceive themselves: their way of life appears to refute them. We cannot know for sure, but our own thinking about doom is different.

The first and still uncertain new fact is that nuclear bombs are apparently barring war between the states that have them. Instead of new wars, the advances in weapons technology are compelling peace. If this initial compulsion were subsequently absorbed into the ethos of nations, the result would be a transformation of humanity.

Whoever thinks about foreign policy today must do it in these terms if he is not to assist in the thoughtless promotion of doom.

The World Situation

In the present world situation the goals of free and rational nations are two. One is world peace, because of the nuclear peril; the other is freedom, because of the threat of total rule.

Peace has always been what a majority of people craved, though not without conditions. Today, for the first time, there must be an unconditional will to peace. The only dissenters are those who would not merely lay down their own lives but would drag their countries and all of mankind down with them. For war is no longer what it was—a last resort that makes sense in extremity. Since its destructiveness has become absolute, war is now senseless.

Freedom is a road to be pursued first within the nations. Political freedom is a responsibility of all citizens. It takes conviction and dependable political morality. It bars violence and seeks constantly renewed communication. Only nations that achieve domestic political liberty are capable of alliances with other free nations, because they are ready to solve all problems by agreement rather than by force.

Thus far, however, only a very few nations are taking this road, and violence and totalitarianism are realities that threaten everyone else in the world. The burning question is how world politics looks in fact.

POLITICAL REALITIES AND CRITERIA OF ACTION

Today no nation and no state can separate its interests from those of mankind at large. No nation is safe if the existence of mankind is threatened. At a time when travel round the globe is as simple as a journey of fifty miles used to be; when all events are connected by the omnipresent daily news; when national leaders can arrange to meet as quickly as if they were fellow townsmen; when military strategy has become global strategy—at such a time each state, each nation, must consider what effect its actions will have on the whole.

Everyone must think beyond his temporary individual success or advantage. Every step requires him to ask: Will it work for peace, or does it contain elements that jeopardize the peace? Will it advance political liberty, or does it contain elements of antilibertarian self-will?

And yet, in fact, all states that can arm are arming now, more than ever. Failure to do so puts one in danger of falling prey to another. And today, far too often, the veil of secrecy covers intrigues and schemes against freedom, the construction of legal and institutional roadblocks to political liberty.

Nothing is to be accomplished by making demands of mankind; there is no mankind yet to receive them. We still have to proceed by way of coalescing groups of states that live in political freedom and whose self-preservation implies the salvation—the survival—of mankind.

As yet the idea of "one world" is no moving principle. Some nations, though they talk differently, take themselves for mankind and view the rest as either a field of missionary work, to be infused with their own spirit, or a threat to be met by extermination or enslavement.

A glance at the nations on earth shows only two great powers, the United States and Russia. Great-power status means the factual possession of complete sovereignty, which in turn means the sole decision about world war. All the rest can wage only local wars.

But in the foreseeable future, unless the two take preventive action in time, a third great power will arise in China.

The nations of Europe do not possess this sovereignty. They no longer are great powers. This is the historic change due to World War I, that fratricidal conflict in which Europe, ruler of the world and only center of world history, performed her definitive abdication. It is no longer up to European nations whether or not to risk a world war, nor can they achieve the world peace that can be brought about by the tacit American-Russian accord. The national states of Europe can wage local wars in the shadow of the great powers, with the great powers' permission. Such wars would be murderous and senseless but need not imperil mankind. The European states can set examples: for good if they develop their inner freedom or for evil if they fail their own great past.

Not even a united Europe could be a great power. But a Europe in league with the United States would keep the balance of world history tipped Westward, provided this grand alliance could make common cause in dealing with the other world.

What is it that draws nations together? And what drives them apart? So long as the "one world" idea does not serve as a bond the most far-reaching sympathies are cultural and religious. The West continues to be molded by its biblical and Greco-Roman foundations, the Asian world by its Buddhist and Hindu roots, the Moslem world by its Islamic origin. We are bound by descent from shared cultures and common mores.

Race will tell, whether men are white, black, or yellow. We may try to get away from it; we may even deny that it exists. And yet the racial instinct turns ever more into a font of the fiercest antagonisms. Russia is experiencing this with her guests, the African students in Moscow, and more alarmingly yet, with the Chinese. In America the Negro problem is all but hopelessly complicated by its involvement with economic and social issues. But its solution over there is vital and would point the way for the world.

The crux is the will to political liberty. On this issue there is no middle ground. In principle, for all their "liberalization," the totalitarians remain the same men who built their states, unless an about-face to freedom should some day occur in their political principle. And the free remain on their way to a liberty they cannot reach, in constant peril of some day executing their own about-face to totalitarianism, as the Germans did in 1933.

CHANGED DIPLOMACY AND FINAL GOAL

It is a mistake to assume that foreign relations today might be conducted globally on the same level, as if all states were of a kind. In their dealings with each other they are far from dealing with their kind.

Even the alliances of Western nations vary in character, owing mainly to the implicit motivations that make them more or less firm, more or less lasting. National opportunists tend to exploit situations of the moment, guided solely by nationalistic ambition and vanity, regardless of the community of free nations on which their own very existence rests. It seems that de Gaulle with his romantic illusions would not hesitate, if he could, to tie up with Russia or China in the manner of a bygone age, as Louis XIV would ally himself with the Turks then threatening to inundate all Europe.

One sign of the radically altered world situation is the transformation of diplomacy since the emergence of Bolshevism. The manners shown, the ways of action and propaganda prac-

ticed by the representatives of total rule have closed the common ground peculiar to previous diplomacy. This diplomacy is
still going on between the old powers, but it will fail in dealing
with totalitarians. Their frankly destructive intent, the
effectiveness of their positions, their boundless brutality coupled with talk of peace and justice—all this shows an opponent
what is at stake and fools him at the same time, because he hates
to believe it and does not mind being fooled. We like to talk of
an enigma when we do not want to know what these powers
are really after. We view them as more mysterious and more
astute than they are. Besides, for a while and in certain cases
they like to assume the language and forms of the old diplomacy, only to shatter them the more ruthlessly later.

The old forms have become a superficial sham. Getting the
new totalitarian powers back into them is out of the question.
It would mean restoring a common ground that used to exist
within the West alone, a ground which even then did not
extend to dealings with colonial peoples and "savages." That
diplomacy itself was consummately untruthful; Machiavelli
saw through to its realities. For the future it has no chance.
Now that we are in extremity, facing the naked threat of total
annihilation, a different truth is at issue.

The basic concerns of long-range policy-making are not the
accumulation of material goods for the moment or the present
happiness of consumers whose existence seems secure. Instead,
in the present situation those basic concerns are the goals that
arise from the uncertainty of life itself: freedom and peace.

The final goal can only be mapped out as an idea. It would
be the peaceful union of mankind by manifold, multifarious,
and ultimately all-encompassing agreements between all nations. It would be desirable to have as many small nations as
possible, with a certain minimum size exacted by the
economics of technology while an upper limit is required for
all to remain free. The details of such a possibility could only

be abstract constructions based on geographical facts, on present effects of past history, on technological aspects. No one can predict the form it would take, and what would be politically desirable can be stated only in negative terms. No world state. No world parliament—a road that could not fail to lead to dictatorship and total rule. No world police—a central power that would seize and exploit the factual monopoly on force inherited from the disbanded armies. What would be possible and desirable is a network of agreements tying mankind into a factually peaceful but perpetually unstable confederation. (I have written about this in chapter 7 of my book *The Future of Mankind.*)

There is no lasting condition that might be our final goal. Man is a temporal creature who lives by changing both his world and himself.

PROVISIONAL GOALS

One provisional goal is the coalition of the present free world for the purpose of holding its own by a common foreign policy toward the other world. The coalition must be open to whatever additional nations freely meet the necessary terms—nations in which democracy, constitutionality, and legality are graven upon the citizens' hearts and can be trusted.

The political détente in Europe has so far had two results. The satellite countries are now enjoying a certain limited independence, although as a whole they are as firmly in Russian hands as before. In Western Europe, on the other hand, nations reduced in size and power are prematurely discounting the Eastern threat and virtually ignoring what impends in China. Their rush to resume aspirations to national independence, glory, and self-interest in nineteenth-century style impairs the self-preserving solidarity of the free world. This continuing fission of Europe began in Britain and France; the Federal

Republic, initially quite serious about thinking in European rather than national terms, merely followed suit.

Another provisional goal is an accord between America and Russia on the one point of banning the possession of nuclear arms by any other country. Why? *The issue is paramount because of the possibility that mankind may be wiped out.* The first judgment to be made about our every political act is whether or not it increases the danger that atom bombs will be used.

At present we have some assurance that America and Russia do not want to fight a nuclear war and risk committing double suicide. They are the only two superpowers; on purely economic and technological grounds their atomic arsenal cannot be matched by others in the foreseeable future, and their head start keeps growing. The two giants' resolve to refrain from nuclear war, evident on the occasion of the Cuban missile crisis, was like a turn in world history. And a conventional war between the two has become just as unlikely, since it could not help turning nuclear in the end.

Today the atom probably remains a threat only because there are countries that have smaller bombs—France, Britain, China—and because additional countries are planning to produce them. Such bombs, of course, could not accomplish anything against the superpowers, but upon smaller ones they might inflict frightful damage. The larger the number of small countries that have the bomb, the greater the menace—first, because of the added places in which the fateful decision might be made, and second, because a small country constantly threatened with annihilation by its neighbors (like Israel, for instance) will have a diminished sense of responsibility for the course of history at large. Confining nuclear arms to two powers would reduce the threat immensely. Hence the current tendency to seek agreements that will prevent any more countries from making atom bombs or obtaining them elsewhere. The object is "nonproliferation."

It has been argued on the American side that giving nuclear arms to allies, or sharing nuclear responsibility with allies, does not constitute proliferation. This is simply not so, and the Russians are right to oppose the thesis. Neither Poland nor the Federal Republic should be allowed to have nuclear arms at their disposal, or to have a hand in disposing of such arms.

The effort to reach universal agreement on nonproliferation has so far been unsuccessful. Many countries would be willing to forgo the bomb if Russia and America did the same, but this is unattainable. The bomb exists and cannot be abolished. Even if the two scrapped their whole arsenal it would continue to exist potentially, reproducible in case of war.

Abolition would have a chance only if the vision of Isaiah came true and swords were turned into plowshares. Some day, perhaps, men will get to the point of saying with one voice, "We will discard our arms; we can do without arms, for our lives and actions have become those of new men, of brothers." But that day is too remote to figure in political considerations.

If the goal of limiting the possession of atom bombs cannot be reached by agreement, it can only be reached by a ban. And this could be imposed only with overwhelming nuclear power—in other words, by Russia and America in concert, not by either one acting alone.

A nuclear arms ban by the two superpowers would be an act of force even if enforceable without the use of force. It would be a unique act of force, not to be compared with any other.

Putting it into effect would at the present time involve three countries: Britain, France, and China. Britain, closely tied to the United States, would probably go along at once without trouble. France presumably could be induced to comply by political and economic means, and China, faced with overwhelmingly superior power, might well give in and dismantle her nuclear plants and storage depots voluntarily. If not, the Big Two would have to consider other means to reach the goal. As a last resort—with ample warning to permit evacuation—the plants and depots might be razed by joint Russian-American bombardment.

The premise is an American-Russian accord. Without this accord such logical constructions are invalid. Their purpose is political orientation; they are not programs to be carried out today.

CHINA

The West, a hegemonically structured coalition of free nations for the pursuit of a common foreign policy, faces other nations who do not care for such self-preservation in common freedom. Theirs is the contrary aim of ruling mankind. The principle of their political existence is the tendency to destroy or subjugate. Chinese leaders have stated it in metaphorical terms: their regime was built as the country—the peasantry—conquered the cities, and this is how in a Chinese-led world revolution the "country" of Asian, African, and South American peoples would, and should, overcome the "cities" of the European and North American West (tacitly including Russia). The Chinese have no doubts about succeeding. They have time. They can wait. They worry only about prudent tactics, and to get past their period of relative impotence they will refrain from premature attacks on the powers. We remember Hitler's habit of announcing his every act ahead of time, but in a way that would not let people believe such madnesses of a man whose every other word was peace or freedom, or humanity or justice. Similarly, the Chinese today are talking of the splendidly pacific "principles of Bandoeng."

I am referring to totalitarian China, to the new giant who

rose at the Soviet Union's rear at the very time the Russian menace receded. The Chinese threat to the world seems graver now than the Russian ever was. But what we see is always a specific situation at a particular point in time; analyses and proposals will not remain valid and do not apply in general. Critics of my brief remarks on China in the original German edition of this book have failed to note my hopeful expectation that conditions there will change. I do not regard the present situation as final.

I have been criticized for denigrating the Chinese as somehow still inferior. The contrary is the case. In the Nazi years, when I occupied myself intensively with translations of Chinese literature, I sometimes came to feel at home there, in the East, and a stranger among my own Germans who were driving me to despair. Like everyone who has glanced at their three-thousand-year history I consider the Chinese one of mankind's most civilized nations, and their culture as sublime.

But the present situation there is monstrous. Experts report that an entire tradition is being forcibly crushed, banished from schools, rooted out of libraries. The demolition of China's old "universist" culture is far advanced, and what sort of new construction will replace it is as nebulous as the foundation—the writings of Mao—upon which it will rest. Hence the ambiguity, the sense of strangeness and unpredictability, the surprises. No one knows what to expect.

Chinese totalitarianism is determined to change man himself. In scope and form it far exceeds the worst we know from Russia. The present "cultural revolution" is a full-fledged attempt to stamp out any and every tradition—to let man make a fresh start, to begin all over from his origins, so as to found the only just society. The goal appears to be a prehistoric state of man.

If we want to discuss this we must give free rein to our imagination. No forecast can be based on things we know. A partial discontinuance would be nothing new in China: it was there, in the third century B.C., that the first book burnings in history took place, designed to create a wholly new body politic with a new human mentality and accompanied by measures and official speeches that remind us of modern totalitarianism. But those book burnings were limited to the literature of Confucianism. All other writings were spared and used to support the new state, and many Confucian books too were saved in scattered copies. Even with the violent means of modern technology a complete uprooting of tradition would take a long time.

But let us assume the eradication were successful. We can scarcely visualize the kind of men it would leave. Would they possess the biological traits of a zoological species rather than the human features they would have yet to acquire? One anthropological school regards the Cro-Magnon men of some 25,000 years ago as the first type comparable or identical with ours, and they already had a rich culture. Can man be reduced to that zero point before he turned human? We cannot even imagine such a thing. But what will it mean, then, for Chinese humanity to be reduced to a minimum from which to rebuild man proper, in the proper technological environment? Will it mean a race from the Stone Age, with a Stone Age mentality, but wielding atom bombs and technological equipment instead of stone tools?

Man never exists as nothing. But as what then? What will come out of this "cultural revolution," this extermination drive carried out by juveniles? Who wants it? Who controls it? Does anyone? Does it represent any way of life at all, a will to be in any way human? Or are the Chinese engaged in a dreadful act of self-destruction, an act that threatens to destroy mankind at the same time? Or does their self-destruction mean that we need fear them less?

To me it seems that those interpretive observers who do not fall into traditional clichés are at an utter loss.

The thing upsets all political judgments and counsels. All possibilities, even those no one has ever thought of, must be reckoned with. Nothing seems stable in China. We have seen abysmal plunges and then again achievements of supreme energy, of physical labor and of an industry that makes atom bombs. And increasing the threat is the fact that the Chinese in power seem to know little about the rest of the world and to entertain misconceptions.

In the German version of this book I raised two questions. Must China necessarily turn herself into this fundamentally totalitarian and imperialist power, this menace to mankind? Or is it possible—so long as her words and deeds threaten all other nations on earth, including her would-be consorts in conquest—to isolate China and thus prevent her from realizing her global-imperialist plans? And I suggested two requirements of such preventive action: an economic quarantine and the elimination of China's nuclear capacity.

As a result I was accused of telling the Americans to hurry up and bomb and destroy the Chinese bomb plants—in other words, to risk World War III, since Russia would never stand for this act of destruction. I never dreamed of suggesting any such nonsense. Instead, I am thinking of the chance of a day to come, when an accord between America and Russia will have created the premises on which those two might jointly resolve to save mankind by a worldwide nuclear arms ban.

The realities of today are clear. Technically, if the free world is of one mind in the will to reduce China's capacity for violence, it can be done. But the present lack of solidarity in the free world's will to self-preservation makes it extremely improbable that it will be done.

The accord between America and Russia, the additional

element required for the execution, is now a fact, though not yet in operation. It may take so long to take effect that it will be too late. At present the idea is utopian.

My critics say that to the rest of the world an alliance between the United States and Russia must seem most undesirable, for all others would become dependent, then, upon those two. The world's ball and chain would not be an imperialist pax Americana; it would be a pax Russo-Americana.

This fear is justified. We can put up with it only because of the need for world peace. But the fear is tempered by the expectation that the superpowers would ally themselves to meet the Chinese threat, not to enslave others. Their rivalry would prevent the enslavement of others, and in time the communication of all nations would relax the tension between the small ones and the Big Two. It would be confined to the superpowers' sole responsibility for the atom bomb and for peace; in all other respects there would be an increasingly pluralistic community of independent nations.

Nothing is certain, but world peace is preferable to the end of mankind, unless that peace would end all liberty and every chance for a life that is worth living. With a pax Russo-Americana this risk seems small.

THE FOREIGN POLICY OF SMALL NATIONS

The price that must be paid for the salvation of mankind is high: the two nuclear powers will practically rule the globe. But two facts will keep them from using this mastery to suppress the rest: first, that they are two and will curb one another, and second, that both are largely saturated and need no conquests, having plenty to do on their own vast undeveloped territories.

Even then there could be no definitive peace. Man is not granted such peace. And if he were, he would have reached the end of his possibilities; in a stable state he would cease to be truly human. All our goals are provisional, including those that look like final goals.

In a world situation in which two great powers alone are sovereign, are currently keeping the peace in fact, and will probably—though never certainly—keep it in future, the question is what a small nation's foreign policy can be if it wants to serve peace and freedom and thus to save itself.

It must attach itself to one of the two great powers. There is no other protection for it.

It must deal with its protective power as an ally. The great power and the nation it protects must come to trust each other, to depend on one another. In the relationship between totalitarian state and satellite this is difficult or impossible; it is possible, though not easy, in dealing with the United States.

There is no neutrality any more. No neutral country today can protect its neutrality without armed force. Since the rise of Russian Bolshevism and German Nazism neutrality is no longer respected anywhere. It is violated at will or admitted for a time, on practical terms, if it benefits the aggressor.

For small nations war and peace are decreed from outside. They can make war on their own only if the great powers will abet or permit it, and then only locally, with conventional weapons. A world war would come today only—but then certainly—if the United States and Russia were to fight each other.

The vital question for the small nations of Europe is whether a European war can be localized, as could thus far be done with others round the globe. The armaments and other war preparations of the Europeans depend on the answer to this question. A local European war is improbable because, unlike a war anywhere else, it would involve America and Russia from the outset. Neither one can afford to leave Europe to the other.

But we cannot rely on the Europeans to keep still. There

was a time when violent actions by East Germany against West Berlin seemed imminent, and they would have occurred if the Americans had not been on the spot. And if military tendencies should win out in the Federal Republic, violent actions to regain the former German territories in the East are not impossible. That these could remain localized is most unlikely. American and Russian interests are so deeply involved here that the Big Two will have either to stop a local war or to fight a world war.

The small nations of Europe must not go to war. Even if waged with conventional weapons only, such a war in the present world situation would be madness. It would mean the suicide of the belligerents and probably kindle a world war.

Europeans still live by illusions, in every country. They cling to positions that are past and cannot be regained. The old European nationalisms are inconsistent with the task of Europe in today's world. The policies now pursued by de Gaulle are repugnant and give pause to thinking people. They show how the minds of his German followers work. This romanticism, which imperils peace and freedom, will be tolerated as long as no outright calamity ensues—tolerated out of courtesy to a head of state and out of affection for the French people, their country, and their spirit.

German Foreign Policy

For the Federal Republic as for all European countries, political self-confidence and dignity can spring only from acting within the free world in the interest of common self-preservation. Its own significance is derived from conscious integration in the entirety of the West. In case of conflict the entirety takes precedence.

Our people must be shown the real situation in the world;

again and again, by government, parliament, politicians, and the press, they must have it pointed out and impressed upon them. If this is not done, if things are glossed over, the people have virtually no defense against illusions and idle fancies— unless they should listen to their writers, which they will not. For the writers reach only a very limited audience.

The tendency in the republic, due in part to the ever-increasing wealth of our consumers' economy, is to seek "normalcy" in politics. The effect is to forget the world situation. Activities during a breathing spell are called "normal"; surface facts of the moment are mistaken for the whole reality. These surface facts are then reduced to partisan concerns, to the careers of individual politicians. Politics becomes a maze of intrigue and extortion, with the actual issues lost from sight. Foreign policy is immobilized in blind alleys, entered by unanimous consent; it becomes a policy of unfulfillable demands and achieves nothing of substance. For no great, high-minded, integral policies can evolve unless a view of the worst—which, after all, exists and has already manifested itself—sets their course.

TERRITORIAL BORDERS AND "LEGAL CLAIMS"

What foreign policies are open to the Federal Republic? In the past, defeats and territorial losses have always bred a spirit of revenge. If there was the slightest possibility, real or imagined, losses were to be recouped. But what used to be normal has in a sense become criminal in the nuclear age. Today there is something final about the borderlines that have resulted from past political history. The globe has been distributed. Privileged nations possess vast territories, entire continents; the small ones have to be content with specks of land. The alternative is always the same: world war, nuclear war, the end of mankind. The borders drawn as the result of a war that was unequivocally and unprovokedly launched by Hitler's Reich must be accepted as facts and recognized. This is not a matter of punishment but of force engendering force. When a man has run amuck and had to be struck down, he must take the consequences of running amuck.

And if a man wipes out legality, he cannot later advance "legal" claims based upon a past which is no more. If the victor's mercy lets him live, if the reply to his Auschwitz has not been his own dispatch to a new Auschwitz, he must found his new existence on the facts now given.

The changes in the German borders were caused by the lawless use of German force, and decreed by the victors. Any legal argument we make against them covers a will to resort some day to new force. Rights lost in the paths of force have ceased to be rights. The peace is not menaced by those who hold on to what war has given them; it is menaced by one who demands a restoration of things past. If I want peace I must acknowledge facts that cannot be changed without force.

All citizens answer for the acts of their state, even of a criminal state. This means they have to accept the factual outcome and envision their own future on that basis. Whatever may be "freely and peacefully" changeable can only be approached in a spirit of candor and equity, without legal claims. It can be reasonably discussed, not unilaterally demanded.

The Federal Republic has no legal claims. It is one part of the Germany that was split by decisions of the occupying powers, and this in turn had emerged from the Germany of unconditional surrender. The Potsdam agreement was an accord among the victors; it did not create obligations toward the vanquished. To cite future peace talks and a treaty then to be signed means to take your stand on a delusive fiction. A peace treaty that has not been signed for twenty years will never be signed. There is peace without it.

The war created new facts, and thus new legal premises—not

by treaty, but by the way it came out. There are no rights that sanction these consequences, but the consequences sanction new rights.

The alternative is always one and the same. It lies in the nature of the case that border revisions now sought "freely and peacefully" will some day, when opportunity beckons, be sought by force. Legal claims outside their proper sphere are hostile acts; the will to gain one's "right" by force is hidden only because one still lacks the power.

We voice our claims with the ostensibly resistless vigor of demanding "inalienable" rights. But there are no more rights in a political situation created by force of arms. Whoever rebels against such a situation cites rights from a past to which the war has put an end, while the victor cites rights that entitle him to his victory. A legal argument puts all this on the wrong level. It is not a matter of right or wrong, of title or accusation. The outcome of forcible action leaves only two possibilities: we can want new force, or we can want reconciliation on the basis of actuality.

The false legal claims become barriers blocking any chance of real peace. Peace is threatened, we say in the Federal Republic, because the Oder-Neisse line is maintained, or because we are refused reunification—but then the threat, after all, comes from our republic which refuses to recognize the results of Hitler's acts and every German's political liability for those acts. A potential menace of war is inherent in my will to change a territorial status which others want to maintain. The one who threatens is the one who wants to change existing boundaries, not the one who wants to preserve them.

We must be clear in our minds. We know that leading German politicians call for restoration of the German borders of 1937, that a cabinet member who publicly claims the Sudetenland is not dismissed on the spot, that refugee groups with official sanction and participation demand the return of their homelands—and we must realize that these facts serve not only to provoke our Eastern neighbors but to reinforce their suspicions and to enhance the extraordinary fear of Germany which the past has instilled in them. The consequence is enmity and a desire for protection against Germany. Understandably, these countries cannot forget what they suffered at German hands and what, accordingly, they expect in the future.

To call the failure to achieve reunification a threat to peace can only mean that our republic is threatening the peace. It is pursuing a "policy of strength," intending some day to reach its objective by war, or by military pressures that may lead to war.

The cry for reunification worries every country in Europe, if not the United States. The West Europeans formally back our claim, their minds eased by the knowledge that nothing will come of it anyway. For the East, and also for France, the thought of a Germany reunified into an overwhelmingly superior power is a nightmare.

THE PRINCIPLE OF SELF-DETERMINATION

We base our "legal claim" on national self-determination, a principle acknowledged all over the world. The Russians and Chinese apply it to nationalities outside their domain, not to the ones they deal with, as appeared in Hungary, Tibet, and other cases. The West, including the United States, takes the principle seriously and applies it in good faith to all peoples, white or colored, historically civilized or not. The point of the principle is hardly ever considered.

Originally, self-determination is the right which free men win when they will risk and sacrifice their lives and property to liberate themselves by force from outside force, purporting to found their own body politic on the citizens' liberty. That inner political freedom is what lends strength to their determination to prevail against force. We know this true and splendid self-determination from Swiss, Dutch, British, and American history; in German history we know it from such glorious failures as the Frisian peasants' freedom which took the joint force of emperor and pope to crush, or the civic freedom which the Hanse towns maintained for a hundred years.

Today, however, self-determination is viewed as a human right as such, as every people's due. On the one hand, this "right" is an imposition. There are people still unaware of political liberty and incapable of exercising it; yet this right would require them to be free. It is the same callousness which in the personal life of individuals insists upon another's freedom when he is not up to it yet, when he secretly wants to be taken by the hand and gently guided in the direction of freedom. On the other hand, this right of self-determination comes as a gift to the unfree, who do not know what to do with it—as fortunes won in a lottery, after a period of intoxication, may leave the winners poor as before, and spoiled to boot. The gift will not make such a people free; it will induce them to succumb to dictators and their ambitions, and to butcher each other. It will make them a menace to freedom in the world. The gift of such a "right" of self-determination makes a farce of faith in humanity, a farce in which we forget that it takes freedom to gain freedom and that one has to regain it constantly in dealing with himself. True faith in humanity lies in regarding freedom as the human challenge, not in assuming that the challenge has been met.

Between the grand self-determination and the distorted one lie many possibilities. Above all, there is the matter of population groups voting to decide which state they want to belong to, or whether they want to have their own independent state. Such plebiscites have proved to be peacemaking and therefore justified only in rare instances, when held under neutral supervision (for unsupervised plebiscites tend largely to be managed). A meaningful and successful one took place, with French agreement, in the Saar basin in 1935: the result, an overwhelming majority for union with Germany, left only a small remnant of opponents who were not bothered afterwards. To refuse such plebiscites, as Bismarck did in Alsace-Lorraine and Nehru in Kashmir, may be fatal.

The crux is the definition of the areas in which a majority will decide. This is already an anticipatory decision. If the borders are as clear as they were in the Saar it will be easy; but if they are drawn on military and power-political grounds, not on ethnic or linguistic ones, the outvoted minorities will remain strong and hostile. Where the intermingling of languages and nationalities makes any delimitation impossible there will be constant unrest, enmities, and threats of war, as demonstrated by the Eastern states which self-determination produced after World War I. Any attempt to protect minorities will fail because the idea of political liberty is lacking in the basis of such a state—the idea which in Switzerland, for instance, unites four peoples speaking different languages in one national consciousness.

How does the self-determination principle apply to the reunification demanded by the Federal Republic? To begin with, this is not a case of the heroic self-determination of free men setting out to build a state. Neither West Germany nor East Germany arose from an act of free self-determination. Both were set up from outside, in forms and under rules peculiar to the greatly divergent Western and Russian political mentalities. In the West, at least in the United States, there is self-determination, but the East does not apply it to its factual domain.

The German practice in the past has not been to recognize this self-determination. In Hitler's Reich it was ignored as nonexistent. The centuries-old Prussian, Russian, and Austrian abuse of Poland was pure power politics. It was on grounds of

Prussian power that Bismarck firmly blocked a Polish restoration, and even granting the desirability of this Prussian power in itself, the right to use it in such ways came from the will to power, not from the political ethos of international law.

A self-determining choice of the state one wants to belong to can become practical only if both states in question agree to abide by the result of the vote. In the absence of such agreement the question is not one of right but of political power.

We want a plebiscite in East Germany. (A joint plebiscite in both West and East Germany would be palpably wrong, since the result could be interpreted only as dictated by the West German majority.) But the "right" to such a vote is a question of power; as a legal question it is insoluble because our law is not the law of our opponents. Therefore, unless a general reconciliation should bring the great powers—in this case, America and Russia—into agreement on a neutrally supervised plebiscite, we have actually nothing to say. What we must do in the real situation is to find the most promising ways to expand the personal freedom of the East Germans, and to raise their standard of living. Anything more, any legal claim advanced unilaterally on our part, is a camouflaged will to violence.

THE NEW PREMISES

"Conquering the past" has become a German slogan and the object of much soul-searching and argument. But we do not conquer the past by forgetting it or by feelings of "shame" that imply secret excuses. We conquer it by changing—among other things, by an unreserved admission of the consequences of the war. This means to recognize borders that were drawn by force, to be sure, but by the force of the reaction to an earlier, utterly inexcusable use of force by overwhelming German power. It means that the question raised toward the end of

World War I, "What to do if we lose?" cannot possibly be answered as it was then, by a distinguished German: "Start at once to prepare for the next war."

An admission of the new points of departure brings us to certain inescapable premises of any German policy, provided we want peace.

a) The Oder-Neisse line is final. The land to the east of it is inhabited by Poles, almost half of them already born there, and is now their homeland.

b) The special status of the Soviet zone of occupation is final as long as Russia wants it to be. East Germany is one of her satellites and will remain one as long as the other satellites exist.

Our insistence that these two realities are still negotiable, that acceptance of (*a*) would be an "advance concession" or that (*b*) will never be acceptable—this is what Russia and the satellites not only reject but consider a threat to peace. If we want to live in peace and, as far as possible, in friendship with our eastern neighbors we must not talk of claims whose legality the other side will not and cannot acknowledge, because it does not exist.

The people expelled from their native provinces east of the line have suffered a grievous blow of fate, for the loss of his homeland tears a man's life asunder. I know it not from those Germans alone, but from many German Jews who were driven out of Germany to foreign-speaking havens. They cannot get over the loss; they are not truly at home anywhere. It takes a generation to feel differently: the children of the refugees do have new homelands.

The East Germans' lot is not a happier one. Their lives are hard, the large governing class excepted. They cannot rise to the normal living standards of the modern Western world. They are Germans and fully as good as the Germans in the West, but the economic effects of the Communist system prevent them from attaining the productivity that is possible nowadays. The Russians exploit them, and those of them who care for freedom miss it.

It is plainly unfair. Why should the East Germans suffer, not the West Germans? But such is fate as geography determines it, and the injustice, like so much injustice in the world, cannot be completely eliminated, but perhaps it could be lessened. Instead of vainly calling for reunification, the West Germans today must ask themselves how they might possibly help the East Germans, and do it.

No shrewd diplomatic bargaining methods, no horse-trading, starting with maximum demands and keeping secret what you are ready to give in the end—none of this can bring about a settlement of fundamental questions. What then can we do?

Motivated by a change in our political mentality, we can change the situation by acting so as to lay the ground for developments that will benefit all sides.

The present West German policy serves to depress East German living standards and to prevent the possible liberalization of conditions over there. Real, live Germans suffer for a policy that is supposed to serve imaginary Germans.

We must extend economic aid to East Germany in order to make it as prosperous as possible despite its unproductive Communist regime. The argument against this is that it will only bolster Ulbricht's rule. It will indeed, but we must put up with this bolstering, having no other chance to promote the higher living standards which we owe to our countrymen, our German neighbors. Our present policy of using economic relations with the Eastern zone to put pressure on Ulbricht is futile. It only serves to complete the zone's economic dependence on Russia, and to intensify its exploitation. It hurts the Germans in the East. But the objective of our policy is a mirage, the unattainable reunification; we do not really want to help the Germans in the East.

If we do what we can to promote East Germany's economic recovery we shall be helping more than by our rejection of it, which is so hard on our compatriots—the rejection for which they pay in low living standards and which robs them of the chance of liberalization.

We must forgo reunification, or a "new unification," as some call it now. We must be content with the greatest possible measure of personal freedom and economic prosperity that can be won in the East.

We must work for a possible liberalization so far as we indirectly can, and in line with developments in the satellite countries. Conditions in East Germany are far worse than in Poland or Czechoslovakia. The terroristic curbs on the spoken or written word, on a private life that knows no solitude, no reflection, nothing but constant direction, are obviously intolerable. But this must,be due to special circumstances and is not essential to satellite status as such. East Germany reminds us of life under the Nazis; Poland and Czechoslovakia do not. The policies pursued in Bonn might change the circumstances, though not in some simply calculable way.

We must refrain, however, from direct interference in East German domestic affairs. We must not call on the others to go in for libertarian policies. This is something they will have to do by themselves, without Western demands or interference.

We must distinguish the totalitarian terror that reigned under Stalin and Hitler from a Communist order of government and way of life—from the way of life of our Eastern neighbors, which we must respect as a fact. We are not to give aid to revolutions; we must not even want to aid them.

We must try to promote a common life of the mind in the great, historically given cultural community of Europe, which includes the present Russian satellites.

We must abandon the Hallstein Doctrine. Instead, we must

strengthen economic and cultural ties and develop friendly relations with the satellites, regardless of their recognition of East Germany (granted under Russian pressure, anyway). The Hallstein Doctrine is a shackle we have fastened about our own policy. It springs from abstract, legalistic ways of thinking which effect no change at all in reality but prevent us from achieving possible, desirable changes.

Should we or should we not recognize East Germany? To me this seems to be a matter of timing. As long as the Wall splits Berlin, as long as barbed wire runs along our common border, we cannot recognize East Germany. But if both were to come down as a result of our policies, if the border could again be freely crossed, recognition would correspond to the realities. The Germans of both states would once more be free to associate without desiring to belong to a single, larger state—which is nothing, after all, but an illusion destructive of the political opportunities that exist.

All in all, we must create confidence that the West poses no threat to the satellites or to East Germany.

It will take time, but eventually, perhaps, this course may lead to conditions that would make it seem advantageous to Soviet Russia to withdraw her occupying forces from the satellites. She might come to feel that these nations want to develop their own communism, each in its own way, perhaps, but will not join capitalism in an anti-Russian alliance. Then, in view of the new totalitarian threat of imperialist China, Russia could reach a political understanding with the West as a whole.

The current talk of "small steps"—supposedly exceeded by "medium steps"—seems utterly inane. The supposition in such twaddle is that we are taking any steps at all which might move us forward. This is not the case. What we need is a radical, basic decision which will then take us to very different successful steps.

If we honestly want friendship with the Eastern countries we can have it. The non-German satellites want their own freedom from Russia; they want the Russian troops withdrawn from their soil. They will press their demands when they no longer need to fear Germany. It will take time for us to gain their confidence by demonstrating constantly that our policy has changed.

If we drop our claims we are advancing the one thing that counts: the freedom of the East Germans. In the satellite countries as in Russia proper, life is being liberalized, and under the westward pressure of this factual liberalization East Germany finds herself more and more hard put to keep withholding her own. She is a satellite whose fate is linked with that of all the other satellites; as the others go free, East Germany will grow freer. Russia cannot keep troops in East Germany when she evacuates the rest. The result will certainly not be an East Germany with political freedom in the Western sense, but for all the difference in structure it may be a state that satisfies its citizens and enjoys their support and cooperation.

The satellites and East Germany have a common stake in freedom. The people of those countries do not want Russian rule, or a rule under the burden of Russian occupation forces. All of them will slowly become our friends if we stop demanding what we cannot get in any case—and what after Hitler's war we are not entitled to either.

Only one problem remains insoluble for the time being: neither West Berlin nor the Federal Republic can recognize the Berlin Wall. That monstrous fact whose inhumanity we feel each day is untenable. The only way to make it vanish is to make it unnecessary. If East Germany prospers, if a measure of liberalization ensues as in Poland, people will not be pressing to go west. There will be no new mass migration. Even against the Wall the only promising policy is to give East Germany economic assistance.

A POLICY OF PEACE

In case we recognize the facts and take the consequences—and do so not by occasional half measures but in principle and completely—the chances of peace will have improved immeasurably. Our present claims and demands, on the other hand, doom every chance. They magnify the fear of German madness and of German military power. One who is not satisfied with what he has strikes everybody as an enemy of peace, and indeed he is one. But if a change in Germany were to become a fact beyond doubt, it would not only augment our freedom in the Federal Republic but remove the grounds of Germanophobia. Peace in Europe would be assured.

We hear that the will to reunification is a fact; a whole nation wills it. But a seeming national will is as subject to change by insight as the opinion of politicians. Not subject to change by insight are such facts as geography, the possession of large territories and natural resources, population volume, and the factual control of nuclear arms.

We hear further that if the Russians refuse to permit reunification and declare the Oder-Neisse line to be unalterable, this fact too is just a whim subject to change on the Russians' part, as ours is supposed to be. We need only stand fast, according to this reasoning; if we do not give in they will come to see the light. But the difference is crucial: the Russians want to preserve existing boundaries while we want to change them. The Easterners want to keep what they have; we want what we do not have. But in the present world situation peace requires recognition of the status quo. Nonrecognition itself is a threat to peace.

If we say that Europe cannot have peace until reunification is achieved, this demand in itself is inimical to peace. In past times war was a possibility one could always operate with;

today it has become impossible as a matter of political ethics. This changes all motivations.

The German reunification policy expects help from the Western Allies, although it is nonsensical and the Western powers actually cannot help. That until now they have seemed to be going along with Bonn's line of the "borders of 1937" is a matter of courtesy; in fact they know that these aims are beyond realization. The formula "not until the peace treaty" costs nothing and ties the issue to an event that will never occur. But now the Allies are slowly growing restive. We see the rise of pressures to which the republic will some day have to yield if it does not want to be completely isolated and regarded as a dangerous marplot, an obstacle to a relaxation of tensions and a barrier to world peace.

Gerhard Schroeder made a revealing remark once, when he was foreign minister. "The thought of peace," he said, "has moved ahead of reunification. A reunification policy is getting to be more and more difficult." The answer would be: does reunification matter more than world peace? If peace is tied to reunification, the will to reunification runs counter to peace. "Reunification in peace and freedom" is a phrase; the threat of war is ingrained in the matter. Let us not delude ourselves: in the eyes of the East the demand for reunification is a hostile act. After what has happened—and considering some voices heard in Germany today—can we expect or ask the East to stop being afraid of us unless our Eastern policy undergoes radical changes?

If I throw stumbling blocks into my own path I must remove them before I can proceed, and a policy of demanding both reunification and peace is like the child who wants to have his cake and eat it.

Failure to accept the Oder-Neisse line and give up reunification long ago has brought us to a political dead end. Our foreign policy is not only mired and immobilized but facing a serious, needless, and very harmful defeat.

Today we hear recognition of the Oder-Neisse line favored by men who have always kept silent and are speaking now under pressure, their credibility impaired by sins of omission going back many years. With defeat staring them in the face there is no mistaking the opportunism of their reaction. Those voices are half-muted.

It may not be too late even now if we resolve to go all out, without quibbling or equivocation. Morally and politically our resolution will be ineffective unless it is freely made and radical, extending to reunification also. Nothing else will set us free within. Nothing else will make the satellites our friends. Nothing else will ease the minds of our allies and curb their secretly growing resentment. By making friends with our Eastern neighbors we would preserve ourselves, our possessions, and our potential. We simply must accept the outcome of the war which Germany unleashed, because all Germans, even the innocent, answer as nationals for what the nation has done.

What is dignified and will win friends as a free choice becomes undignified if done reluctantly, under pressure. And it would fail to bear fruit because the fear and distrust of the Federal Republic would remain.

"SECURITY" AND THE UNITED STATES

Every German wants security. Every party, every government will promise him security.

But the word has different meanings in domestic and foreign affairs. At home, with political and personal liberty and constitutional rights at issue, the notion of security is void if it would serve to impair those rights; security measures that crush what they are supposed to secure are absurd. Abroad, in matters of military security, the point is to do nothing and to demand nothing that will impair a small nation's only security, the chance for peace. Our security cannot rest on the peacetime planning and preparedness of a military organization, only on

the policies of the whole Western world. These security policies would be imperiled if the name of defense were used to
shroud violent trends. To cut loose from the overall security of
the West is the wrong way. The maxim "We cannot rely on
anyone but ourselves" is no longer applicable. Like it or not,
we have to rely upon others, as they must rely upon us.

The Federal Republic cannot protect itself, cannot secure
itself, would not be able to defend itself alone against an attack
from the East. Not even with French and British help could it
do so. If there can be security in the world of today, ours rests
with the United States alone. From this fact we must draw our
conclusions. We ought to think about foreign policy questions;
we should give advice; but we must recognize American hegemony. The global interests of the United States are our own.

Pros and cons. This thesis of mine has been violently contra-
dicted.

America, I am told, perpetrates horrors that we cannot go
along with. The Americans consider only their own interest,
and ours only insofar as it serves theirs.

I am accused of trusting them blindly, of expecting them to
side with us for our own sake if we earn their trust.

I am reminded that turning to America will cost us our
sovereignty, which we ought not to give up. Instead, we
should use our strength to seek help where it is offered and
alliances where they are welcome. After all, we do not want to
be a satellite.

Finally, I hear that the American tie would also bring us
closer to the American way of life and of thinking. And we do
not want to become Americanized.

Let us examine these arguments.

Dreadful things do happen in America. It is a country capable of both the best and the worst. It produced a Kennedy as it
produced a McCarthy. It has a Birch Society, a Ku Klux Klan,

juvenile delinquents, unsafe streets, deteriorating cities, bloody excesses. There are corrupt unions over there, and corrupt businessmen. Besides there are objective problems such as the almost insolubly complex Negro question.

It is obviously easy to write books about all that is wrong with America, books of execration and of warning. We read these books to guard against illusions. And yet, in the end we always see the formidable counterforces. What giant efforts to fight seemingly unconquerable ills are made in America! One is not blind there. Men see the evil and act.

The most intense form of the political struggle there is still the struggle of minds. Take the discussion of the Vietnam issue. How serious, how well-informed, on how high a level! In America one finds the freest, the frankest of all men steeped and living in the gravity of the historic situation. We in the Federal Republic are unbearably provincial in comparison.

In the American body politic, for all the madness that will erupt now and then, lies something which no other power in the world has achieved. If we want democracy—and I keep citing Churchill's description of it as "the worst form of government except for all the others"—if we do want democracy under the conditions of today, the American one is farthest from being the worst. (I am not referring to the small European democracies whose good fortune, as long as it lasts, is not to be responsible for the course of world history.)

More than anywhere else in the world, it seems that righteousness, decency, trustworthiness, reason, and helpfulness are facts in that nation of emigrants from almost all nations, the American people.

Kennedy. Nothing has made so clear what America means to us as did the administration and assassination of John F. Kennedy.

Today America alone has brought forth a great statesman.

For a moment—two years—he illuminated our age. Kennedy's sense of reality, his familiarity with current issues round the globe, his knowledge of men, of peoples, of states—these were the foundations of his judgment. He had come to know the state of the world from actual experience, observing and swiftly grasping situations from adolescence on. His total commitment to freedom and human dignity inspired him and, with him, the American people. Not until he went into action as president did his candor in personal contact with the individuals he met, his respect for the powers of the human mind, become fully apparent. Then he developed his magnetic attraction for the people; then he won their trust by pairing courage with cool deliberation under fire. His sense of destiny, neither optimistic nor pessimistic, spurred the American reassumption of global political responsibility as a great nation among free nations.

The goal was peace, but not at the price of Americans and others round the world losing their freedom and their dignity. This was what made the Cuban crisis unique. The risk which Kennedy took, the risk he frankly disclosed to the people and let them share, revealed that Russia and America do not intend at present to wage nuclear war. A different climate has since prevailed in the world (although to those who understand neither Kennedy nor his political thinking he was just "putting on a show"). In America the present president is said to be continuing Kennedy's policies. This does not seem quite believable. Kennedy spoke out strongly against a "pax Americana"; his fundamental, crucial idea for overall United States policy was to reject any hidden American imperialism. Johnson has occasionally spoken favorably of that sort of peace.

One man put a nation back on the track. The echo he found in the depths of the American ethos raised the people themselves to their proper, higher level. The forces of their political morality emerged from hiding. The accustomed power drives, the fierce expansionism, the violent instincts subsided.

It seemed an elemental event in the realm of free political ethics, bound to lead the United States back to its origins by transforming its present condition. This condition had become the field of other powers, the vehicle of their anonymous pursuit and affirmation of everything Kennedy opposed. His personality was the fillip and the cement of this old, new America.

What happened then? It can only be interpreted, not proved. "This is no ordinary enemy," the anonymous ones told themselves, "not one whom time and elections will get rid of. Kennedy is a man, rather, whose personality and political ethics will keep in flux whatever goes with him, whatever will go his way. We who have been running things are through— through while he lives, not only while he is president. The country is becoming a different country that will never again give us a role to play." No intellectual struggle and no political one can eliminate such an embodiment of truth and freedom—nothing but murder. It is a strange case in history that one man can make all the difference. Not until the man is removed will the road be clear again for those other powers. Thoughts like these would bear out the old adage that truth no sooner appears in the world in full earnest than it will be killed.

America could produce this man and raise him to the top; anonymous American powers killed him. It was not only in America that people burst into tears when Kennedy was assassinated, even though as yet there was no clear, political reflection on the import and the consequences of the crime, only an indistinct sense of enormity. It was as if the devil had intervened in history at the very moment of a turn for the better. For two years we had been breathing a new and different air in global politics. And now?

The crime is unsolved. Politically this is almost as fatal as the assassination itself. Thus far the American people as a whole have not mastered the dreadful event.

The most respected, most trusted and unassailable judge, Chief Justice Warren, was put in charge of the investigation. He said that the truth about the murder would not be fully known to the present generation—which could mean only that findings contrary to the national interest would not be made public. Such remarks bear out the confidence in Warren's veracity. They were accepted. I recall only one voice of protest, a private full-page advertisement (in the *New York Times*, if my memory is correct) which said in substance: "Since when has an American judge another duty than to uncover the truth, the whole truth, regardless of anything but the truth? The facts, past and present, should not be hidden from the American people. We want to know what is happening to us."

The investigation resulted in a record of twenty-odd volumes, which were published, and a report. Lawyers prepared to study the twenty-odd volumes were thus enabled to show discrepancies. The record itself made it possible to cast doubt on the final report of the judges.

That the solution of the crime was not pursued as far as possible appeared at first to fit in with a popular mood. Americans realized the alternatives. They could either face themselves and the world as a country in which certain forces wanted such a murder and could get it perpetrated, perhaps even with the aid of government organs. Or they could leave things obscure, an end best served by the official version that Lee Harvey Oswald was a lone assassin acting purely on unclarified private motives—that the crime was an accident. The second course was chosen, with the result that for a while the question remained taboo.

But America is still America. The issue would not stay dead. Several authors published books based on their own investigations of the case. People came to think about it. Publicly no one knows any more as yet; despite the shattering doubts there are even some lawyers who agree with the report and regard Oswald as the sole assassin. But every statement, even this one, is now wavering. Nothing is settled any more. If for three years the American people seemed loath to get to the bottom of the crime, the reverse is apparently true now. The question is discussed again. Nothing is known, but people form opinions. As I write this, the *Herald Tribune* of October 4, 1966, prints the results of a poll: 60 per cent of those questioned reject the conclusion of the Warren Report that Kennedy's assassination was the act of one man. They tend to believe it was "part of a larger plot" although they cannot say who was behind it.

After Kennedy's death Americans seemed to be backsliding into the gray world of purely pragmatic politics. They were about to forget Kennedy. Now this impression is fading also. Kennedy is not dead. He need not be gone and forgotten: his political works, his writings, speeches, and notes, are available. His life stands all but tangibly before us in two biographies. His speeches and works are, or ought to become, the most important field of contemporary political study.

Vietnam. Today the war in Vietnam is the argument for the thesis that we cannot side unconditionally with America—that if we were to put America first we would have to back that war with action, or at least with words. But we need not back it at all, not as it is waged by the present administration. Our friends, the men who make up our America, are the great Americans who stand today against Johnson, the men who urge prompt termination of this atrocious war—which in fact, if not in intention, is nothing but an effort to exterminate a country and its population by every means of modern technology. Vietnam has become the fate that threatens America and us and the whole world, the fate from which rational nations, and the rational men in positions of power, ought to pull back

precisely because they are free. The Vietnam war has set off
the most impassioned debates in the United States itself. There
too we see the forces that would end it.

This is not the place to discuss the Vietnam problem. In
brief, it involves basic questions of Asian and global policy,
above all the question whether and in what forms the United
States must, or must not, maintain its Far Eastern position. The
numbers of people who doubt the necessity of an American
retreat keep shrinking. But equally clear are the high stakes in a
region that includes Japan, Australia, New Zealand, and other
free countries. What will become of them if America with-
draws and leaves the Far East to itself?

It used to be the prevailing opinion that a withdrawal from
Vietnam would cause the United States to "lose face" throughout Asia and bring about a collapse of its position as "protective power." Yet this is far less likely than the evil that cannot
help flowing from a continuation of the war. Even politically,
in the long run, "face" saved by superior force is feebler than
the moral face which American power should show, in con-
formity with America's oldest political ideas.

Here, as in all other areas, we in the Federal Republic may
form our own opinion of American actions, and we may
publicly participate in the struggle within the United States.
Americans will not consider this disloyal. We are bound to
them in common debate. But if a German opposes the war in
Vietnam, as most men do, he may not for that reason oppose
our unshakeable American alliance. The situation always remains the same: American power is the factual premise of our
republic's relatively safe and permanent existence.

Possible and impossible security. Should we turn away from
the United States because for the moment, at least, there is a
falsehood—the taboo of the Kennedy assassination—embedded

in its body politic? Certainly this is as bad as the lies in the foundations of European states, as our insistence that we either never were Nazis or are quite rid of the mentality of those days, or the insistence of the French that France won World War II. But the crux remains that whatever happens to America is happening to us, all but directly. Even the Kennedy assassination concerns us, as does the failure to shed light on all its aspects. We too have a stake in its further clarification, and our burning interest is far more than curiosity.

And we should realize something else: that we live in an age of multiplying worldwide indications that mankind is headed for a monstrous and not distinctly imaginable catastrophe. The only question we can ask at such a time is what the fullest possible use of human knowledge will enable us to do against the catastrophe, in each concrete situation we encounter. He who wants guarantees—which in fact do not exist—helps to bring on the catastrophe. Today, and for as long as we can see ahead, we are tied to America for good or ill. As things stand, if America goes down, our republic will go down as a free country with the chances of such a country. The old type of foreign policy with its diplomacy and its skills has become a matter of secondary but rather dangerous importance. The sense of tranquillity, of business as usual, which for all our talk to the contrary has brought our actions, the things we are doing in the Federal Republic, to a humiliating climax of complete drift—this is irresponsible not only from the standpoint of *Realpolitik* but of political ethics.

What is going on in America, the alarming changes in democracy, the transformations of a mass society under conditions as historically complex as that land has produced them, the growth of lies—all this becomes our fate as well. We want a policy of truthfulness and must therefore have no illusions, not about America either. But if one goes on to ask whether we should depend on such people, on such a country, he is starting out from the wrong premise. For in the realm of matters of existence there is no dependence on anything.

To demand and expect such absolute dependability one must be blind, fearful, and discouraged. For human beings there is no "right" order of the world. There will never be one. America is not a paradise, not an ideal, not a paragon to be copied. The world which men of all times have built in order to live together will always remain an uncertain world. Each of these worlds may fail, even the ones whose foundation and construction seem to offer every guarantee of endurance. Today the future is more insecure than ever, for every country and for mankind as a whole. Nobody knows whether the United States has any future, whether its ethos and policies will bring about the necessary transformations, or whether it will go down. For us America is a chance, not a warrant of future salvation. Our survival is not guaranteed in any case. Men would cease to be human if they were granted absolute, lasting security. They degenerate wherever they believe they have it.

No alternative. And yet, though we cannot depend on anything, we naturally want as much security as can be had. The unquestionable basic fact today, the necessary point of departure for any consideration of security, is that the United States is the one country with the power to provide Germany and the other small nations of Europe with real protection—not absolute protection, but protection within certain limits—from a contingency which is now latent in Russia. This applies to the world situation as it is today. At long range the détente between Russia and America may be of the greatest significance, but we must not forget that to date there has not been the slightest détente between Russia and the Federal Republic. At the moment we need not be fearful of attack, but we must not forget the Berlin blockade and the Hungarian revolution.

The world and we are tacitly counting on quiet in the near future, but we cannot help feeling some disquiet until our own Eastern policy is included in the détente.

Whatever we might wish to substitute for the United States today would be far worse, things being as they are. De Gaulle's romantic fancies and Machiavellian designs hold out no promise of protection for us, considering the scantiness of French political and military power. Besides, we cannot trust de Gaulle. He will use us, praise us, chide us according to circumstances. By tying us to de Gaulle the Adenauer foreign policy has done great harm to the Federal Republic; nothing but a clear, unequivocal turn away from de Gaulle, back to America, would help. The narrowing of Adenauer's world-political horizon began when he failed to appreciate the greatness of Kennedy—a failure that was not surprising in view of the difference between a politician and a statesman. Kennedy sensed it at once and spoke to Germany not in Bonn but in Frankfurt and Berlin.

America alone can offer us a relatively solid footing. Our hopes must be placed in America because right now we have no other hope. "Now" means today and in the foreseeable future, not for all time. If someone said that we are lost without America, we could not and should not accept such a thesis, for the world does not stand still. What is true now is not forever true. But the situation that would allow us to survive an American collapse lies outside our horizon. No present thought can anticipate what our fate would be then and how far it would remain under our control.

For as long as we can see ahead the consequence is plain. To have a good foreign policy, the Federal Republic must know that its existence depends on the United States, and it must make its American alliance a matter of free will, not of reluctance. Our actions, not just our protestations, must make it clear to the Americans that we have no alternative to the alliance; we are bound to them for good or ill by the facts of the world situation, whether we like or not. It is jointly with them, but as the far smaller power, that we want to face the future. Our part is to help them think and to help them act. We should regard the great American debates as our own, should join in them, but not as an opposition.

Our relationship with our American allies involves them and us in debate on a common basis. This debate does not take place between two closed worlds of thought; it cuts across them. America is no more monolithic than the Federal Republic, and contradictions are inherent in such common ground. We hear American words of solidarity with us as well as warnings of overdoing the contact with the untrustworthy Germans. We hear admonitions to reinforce our Bundeswehr; we also hear misgivings lest it grow too strong and its existence cause fatal complications. These disagreements are arguments on the common ground of having joined, or intending to join, in the defense of political freedom.

We must not equivocate, and we must not permit ourselves to be used against America. We cannot say "the United States and France." America comes first, and other alliances come later, qualified by this unconditional precedence. There is still such a thing as loyalty in the world, and loyalty is never one-sided. It is not accounted for but acted upon. If we play up to de Gaulle we are disloyal to America. If we think we can afford it because America needs us, because their own self-interest would oblige the Americans to help us under any circumstances, we are making a politically pernicious and morally reprehensible mistake. Our great, basic policy line must be firm and clear if we want the political security that is attainable. The same is true of national feelings at large, especially in the United States, where the people affect the decisions of government far more than we do. If the Americans as a nation cease to believe in us the alliance will lose its weight.

There is no getting around it: either the United States is the predominant and protective power, unconditionally and entirely, or it is not. We can become worthy of trust, or we can be isolated on a zigzag course that undermines every trust.

HEGEMONY

I repeat: The free world can preserve itself only by joint action, by pursuing one foreign policy toward the rest of the world. And the form of this self-preservation after all the allies have had their say can only be a factual hegemony of the United States.

For years, as long as the Russian threat remained acute, these facts were determining policy in Western Europe. But since the rise of Chinese pressure has put a temporary halt to Russia's westward expansion, since for the moment all is quiet round Berlin, we have a "détente" now, which no sooner set in than the Western powers thought of their old national sovereignties. What shortsighted political folly! They want to be independent of America. They will deal separately with the rest of the world, each acting in his own interest rather than in the common Western interest. The competition for interest and advantage will occasionally pit them against each other, as in the age of colonialism.

But in fact the threat to the free world has not changed at all. China, which has appeared at Russia's back, looks far more ruthless and dangerous even though today, at this moment, the danger is not yet acute.

The Americans stand at the crossroads of their global policy. In the long run, presumably, their Far Eastern position cannot be maintained; the only question is how and where they will retreat—not out of weakness but freely, having shown their strength. In the United States the view is gaining ground that it cannot and should not be a "world policeman," but the common cause of the free world requires barriers against Chinese and Russian expansion. Their location depends on the free nations' will to survive. Because they have this will, the Federal Republic and Berlin both need the American military presence. So does Japan. That the mood in these countries is affirmative, that "Yankee go home" is not a popular slogan, shows their political insight—as the reverse, when it occurs, is evidence of national obtuseness. Australia and New Zealand are in jeopardy. How the United States will withdraw from the territories of the unfree, where its presence is indeed unwanted, is a question of method, of particular steps and situations.

The Federal Republic will be acting in its own interest if it attaches itself to the global interests of the United States. Should America and Russia impose a nuclear arms ban on all other countries, it would be in our interest to agree. We would be involved as allies and friends; the Big Two would not be "going over our heads" but over the heads of all nations. The Russian-American differences on every point of political freedom and the simultaneous need for their coexistence—no longer a mere phrase but entirely credible now, after China's appearance—assure us that our domestic policies, our education, our intellectual life, our mores and our way of life will be left free and up to us alone.

This must be made emphatically clear. The coalition of free countries under American hegemony is necessary for the survival of freedom, but the alliance affects only their foreign policies toward the unfree world. Each state, each nation, must keep its domestic freedom. Besides, there is a common "domestic" policy of the free world as a whole, principally in economic matters, to which no hegemony can apply. Conflicts must be possible in this area, to be settled by negotiation as within each member country, and unilateral action in case of differences cannot be forbidden even to the smallest. Any such action is extremely dubious, however; in an alliance whose foreign relations are characterized by the hegemony of one, the right approach to matters of common concern is by way of consultation and agreement.

We cannot be world citizens as yet. But we can, in a sense, be citizens of the community of free nations. If we have this feeling, our common interest in the survival of freedom will take precedence over any particular national self-interest.

One form of seeking independence of America is the pursuit of a United Europe that might uphold its sovereignty against the United States and evolve into a "third force" between America and Russia. And indeed, all true Europeans wish for an economic and political integration of Europe, for a conquest of its various nationalisms. So do the Americans. They would be more reliably and unequivocally leagued with a United Europe than with many small states constantly at odds with one another. But Europe would not become a third independent great power able to hold its own. Even a United Europe could be sure of existing only with the United States.

NUCLEAR POWER

The two nuclear powers as the only true great powers have to be distinguished from all other countries. It is a distinction which those others tend to deny.

The split among the West Europeans, and between them and the United States, began with the discovery of a change in American plans. The Americans, we noticed, had given up their previous intention to respond with atom bombs to the first Russian foray against Berlin; they wanted time to try to avert nuclear war, although during this time the Allied troops stationed in Germany plus the conventionally armed ones of the Federal Republic would be no match for the superior Russian forces. This situation seems to be changing now, with the Bundeswehr strengthened. There are many places on earth where frightful wars are being waged with conventional arms, without atom bombs, and in similar fashion we might now be dragged into a cataclysmic local war in which Russia would refrain from using atom bombs, and America from effective intervention.

It is no wonder that the Federal Republic would like a part in the employment of the atom bomb. The nuclear deterrent shields us from the ravages of a conventional war as well, so we want to be able to wield it ourselves. Every country without nuclear arms has this problem.

The problem seems insoluble. There is no way to combine the restriction of nuclear arms to two powers—which is mankind's protection from nuclear war—with a share in the autonomous security enjoyed by a nuclear power. There is no bridging the gulf that divides the Big Two, the only sovereign powers in the full sense of the word, from all other countries.

The gulf would be only partially bridged by America's offer to consult with them about using the bomb. The allies would have a voice, but it would not amount to a share in the final decision; this will always be made by the nuclear power alone. If we were attacked and destroyed by Eastern armies using conventional arms it would be possible for the United States to reject our appeal for a nuclear response, considering any nuclear war suicidal. To be left to the chance of conventional wars is the fate of non-nuclear powers. The nuclear ones must not fight each other and do not intend to. Their privilege is our security. Against third parties they, too, can use only conventional arms.

A nation's wish for nuclear arms of its own is understandable. Its only hope for security seems to lie in the possession of this deterrent—assuming it were really strong enough to deter the giants. Yet if the wish were granted it would only add to the insecurity in the world, because so many countries cannot be trusted. Ruled by a Hitler, for instance, they might go berserk and act nonsensically, trying to bring everyone else down with them. Our own experience of the Nazi period will not so soon let us trust a German state enough to exclude the possibility.

The largest measure of security for all lies in the restriction of nuclear arms to two powers and in the alliance for the self-preservation of the free world.

The insurmountable defect, from our viewpoint, is the risk of becoming involved in conventional wars without sufficient American protection. There are only two antidotes: first, our own strength in conventional arms, which will give pause to a possible aggressor, and second, the assurance that we will not be the aggressors under any circumstances, no matter how tempting the situation and how insistent our generals. This assurance can only be gained in a free and democratically minded country, with secrecy held to a minimum and the people's part in all decisions raised to a maximum.

CONCLUSIONS

We shudder when we look at the world situation. But it is our situation. To deal with it as if it did not exist is cramping and surely pernicious; to see the changes and the chances in it kindles hope and encourages free intervention.

Let me repeat the basic facts.

1. We have caused the war and lost it, at the very moment in world history when war as such has come to pose an unprecedented threat of total extinction. There must be no more war. Morally and politically, therefore, we are obliged to accept the results of the war which Germany unleashed. Unless we do, we are the enemies of peace.

2. Our territory is small and will come to feel smaller and smaller as technological progress continues to spur develop-

ment of the resources of the large continents. The Federal Republic's present position as an economic power next to the Big Two is limited in time; it is no point of departure for policies looking to a more distant future.

3. We have no nuclear arms and are not going to have any, not in the sense in which America and Russia have them. At the most, we might succeed in having them handed over to us under constant American control, with their use dependent on American decisions. We may be given a voice in nuclear questions; we may be consulted in full; but we can never have the right to make independent decisions and choices of our own.

4. We live in peril of invasion and destruction from the East, whether Russian or Chinese, and cannot protect ourselves on our own. Only the United States can protect us.

But since the Russians have intercontinental missiles and can destroy American cities, American nuclear power will never again be used except in case of a threat to the United States itself. The Americans will not risk nuclear annihilation to defend Germany, or Europe. Hence the concept of a "flexible response" to any Russian strike at Berlin, at West Germany, at Europe—the idea of a pause, a waiting period, a chance to contain the advance by political means.

There is no getting around the fact that in the end we are defenseless if the United States will not risk its existence for ours. No force that we might muster can give us protection. Our military preparations can make sense only within the framework of overall American planning.

Of course, we want safeguards against Eastern aggression. We call it "unbearable," for instance, to have to rely on unreliable foreign protection. We say we must be able to defend ourselves; having no atom bombs of our own, we need the right to decide about their use; without this right we are helpless.

But the fact of the matter is that we lack the capacity for autonomous self-preservation. We cannot help remaining dependent on the United States. Even if we have a voice and are consulted, the final decision rests with the United States alone.

5. From the viewpoint of the allied Western world the outbreak of a European war would turn the Federal Republic into an outpost of the kind East Prussia was for Germany in 1914. East Prussia then had to be temporarily abandoned and became a battlefield. The same fate would probably befall the Federal Republic, but in far more cruel a form. As a combat zone and battlefield West Germany might be wiped out altogether.

What can we do for our security?

1. We can pursue an all-out policy of peace, not just in words but in confidence-inspiring action.

2. We can have an alliance with the United States that is not subject to any kind of restriction. We must act so that insofar as our conduct is concerned America will trust us without reservations. Every other tie must be subordinated to this crucial one. And if in time trust should give way to friendship, we still cannot ask our friends to commit suicide for our sake—but we can expect that their policy-makers will try to keep the worst from happening and that we will not be forgotten by their planners. We ought to point out how unprotected we are, so that the Americans will do whatever they can to help us, with our own assistance, by military planning and political advice.

To refuse to take note of these facts is blindness; to plan and act as if they did not exist is madness.

We cannot change the situation of the world, nor that of the Federal Republic in the world. In these situations we must find our living pattern.

We shall destroy ourselves if we try to escape from the supposedly "unbearable" by insisting on the unattainable, on demands inconsistent with peace, and on the "inalienability" of certain claims upon the East.

We must content ourselves with the possible. We can aim at freedom in our body politic, which is up to us, and we can aim at peace, to which we can make major contributions. We must forget about expanding our power, for the essence of our situation would remain unchanged. We can never regain the status of a great power.

We must integrate ourselves. Having definitely lost what used to be called sovereignty, we must consciously do without it. There is dignity in resignation, whereas unfounded claims are mendacious and ridiculous.

Kicking against the pricks, simply aiming at something else that one would wish for, is undignified. We should be too proud to dissemble.

We have to live with a sense of total jeopardy we can do nothing about. The mood it takes is unlike that of trivial bliss or abysmal fear; it is one of preferring life in truth to life under delusions.

We want our fate to have meaning. Men can grow in stature by resigning themselves to historic reality.

VII

SUMMARY AND

OUTLOOK

The course of German policy, both foreign and domestic, cannot be reversed in one detail or another. If the change is to succeed it must be total. There is no point to isolated parts.

The liberty-born, self-liberating policy we should pursue means that the democratic state of free citizens must become a fact. It means there must be checks and balances throughout and unqualified public information. This policy would be against authoritarianism and dictatorship and would do without "internal emergency" legislation. It would not let us militarize people's lives. It would create a spirit of civic action, of an independent but responsible personal existence. It would teach men to think and would require faculties of judgment.

A foreign policy of this sort would work for peace on the basis of acknowledging the consequences of Hitler's war. It would be unequivocal and trustworthy. Freedom and peace are inseparable, and both are impossible without veracity.

A political concept can only be formed as a whole; in

specifics it must be in flux, moving with the world situation. Principles remain the same, but in particulars we have to find new patterns in line with the technological, industrial, and social evolution. And the principles become clearer as insight and will are growing in the people and in their leaders.

The Federal Republic has mired itself in a world of fancies which it founds on legal claims. It has reached the end of a blind alley. It can get out only by a full turn, by reflecting on the real facts and resting its policies on a basis that will support them and is not fictitious.

Political action in our republic proceeds from case to case, without any guiding idea. We set ourselves the wrong goals; we want to be clever; we submit to blackmail; we expose ourselves to humiliation after humiliation and quickly forget each one. Having neither a concept of the world situation nor one of the structure of a republican state, we are neither realists nor freedom-lovers. We are reacting, not acting. We bow to coincidences instead of using them to substantial political ends. All this is mindless and lacks political character.

We are getting nowhere with the web of lies at the core of our national existence. I have tried to show its ramifications: the reference to baseless legal claims; the denial of liability for Hitler's war; the misconception of the significance of unconditional surrender; the notion that we have become new men who must be trusted, and that we really were not Nazis at all. We demand the 1937 borders which we cannot possibly obtain; we hush up the dangers inherent in the fact of our rearmament and in the plans for emergency laws; we tolerate irresolute drift as well as the schemes of ruthless power-seekers; we react far too seldom when constitutional rights are violated or restricted or ignored. Not until the truth prevails can we have a policy; as it is, we just keep muddling through the polluted air that substitutes for our missing political consciousness until outside events brutally intervene. All this would change only if our politicians, and thus our government, were to undergo the kind of transformation that liberates from fictions and leads to the pursuit of positive and realistic goals—goals that inspire the actors and those who think along with them, goals that overshadow personal ambitions and feuds.

I believe that, measured by reality and by the will to freedom and peace, what I have shown is logically compelling, however absurd it may seem in the face of current German views. But what is now rejected as unrealistic might in short order become self-evident if many people were thinking along the same lines. I know I am not saying anything new. Germans are not too stupid to see simple truths, but they tell them to each other only in private. It was that way under the Empire; it was that way in 1918 (when Max Weber alone referred to our so-called revolution as a "bloody carnival" and could not print this in the *Frankfurter Zeitung*); it was that way under the Weimar Republic and under the Nazis (who provided the additional excuses of terror and mortal risk). And now it is that way again.

Truth demands risk-taking. There can be no great policy without risks. Risks are irresponsible when they become adventurous gambles, but the taking of truly responsible risks is the premise of any purposeful political course. Parties and politicians must stake their existence on the achievement of insight, on the spread of guiding convictions, and thus on the creation of a thinking popular will in each concrete instance. They cannot otherwise succeed in developing policies that will profit the people and the nation. Patience in judgment and action is the test of confidence in long-range victory by way of truth.

"Safety first," say our politicians, in all parties. This is evasive. Such men lack the calling for politics. They have no sense for what is latent in the people and will slumber on until, perhaps, some mania rouses them to new irrationality, new dreams, new self-destruction.

Any German who has grown to old age has seen it happen twice, in 1914 and in 1933, and fears it might happen a third time. There is an uncanny permanence in all phenomenal change. Only those Germans who become aware of it can overcome it.

POSTSCRIPT 1967

The German edition of this book contained a postscript written in November, 1965, after the landslide victory of Ludwig Erhard's Christian Democratic government. The election gave that morally unstained, politically pitiable man more power than he could handle; today, in January, 1967, Erhard has become politically nonexistent, replaced with a Kiesinger-Brandt government by the triumphant "grand coalition" of Christian and Social Democrats.

The chancellor of a year ago regarded himself as Germany's God-given savior, beneficial by his mere existence; the question was what, if anything, he would do in the face of strong and diverse opposition within and without his party. Today the question is what the coalition will do with its absolute power, unhampered by any opposition.

The import of the upheaval which the Kiesinger-Brandt regime has wrought in the Federal Republic is difficult to overestimate. Viewed against the background of our previous "democracy," it can lead to grim conclusions. Could this exchange of a decaying democracy for a sort of enlightened absolutism (without the arbitrary power of a princely despot)—could this be the relatively best? However hard to take for anyone thinking along liberal and democratic lines, it may seem preferable to a democracy that is no democracy. If economic survival under a formal government of laws were all that mattered it might be the best solution.

Foreigners may believe that in Kiesinger-Brandt they are now dealing with one united Germany, with all of Germany. One French commentator, François Bondy, actually hailed that government as democratic, an equivalent of Churchill's World War II cabinet of national union! A man taking this incomprehensible view forgets that Britain was then in a crisis, that all energies had to be massed and directed toward saving the nation's existence, that Churchill chose and changed his cabinet, held extraordinary powers but stayed under parliamentary control—a control he sought himself, considering Parliament the guarantee of liberty, the index of public opinion, the arena in which he found jousting a joy, not a hindrance. He won the war but lost the next election, probably because the British wanted no mistake about the origin and purpose of his wartime rule. Having made it clear that they would accept a dictatorship in wartime but not in peacetime, and certainly not for a lifetime, they later elected him once more.

The favorable judgments on the Kiesinger-Brandt regime are born of political despair, but at the same time they suggest a feeling that this government may long endure. More: it seems vindicated in advance by its good luck. At the very outset the new Rumanian tie fell into its lap, a most important item in our foreign policy and the fruit of efforts carried on under Erhard. While the hesitant, cautious old government had advanced it with difficulty, the new one quickly resolved to push it through and to embark upon an active Eastern policy. When merit turns lucky its time has come.

What, then, is the upheaval? It has three aspects.

One: by definitively abolishing an already dwindling opposition, our democracy has abolished itself.

Two: the new system feigns a nonexistent German unity.

Three: our new chancellor is an ex-Nazi.

I should like to quote from two open letters written, before the establishment of the grand coalition, by our one political writer who cannot be praised highly enough, Günter Grass. There may be others of his type, but I do not know them. Grass has shown true independence and does not play the pundit; in strong, plain language without literary frills he speaks out on events of the day.

"I want to make a last, fully public attempt to move you to reconsider," he wrote to Kiesinger. "How are we to remember the tortured, murdered resistance fighters and the dead of Auschwitz and Treblinka if you, the fellow traveler of those days, dare now set the guidelines of our policy? What history is to be taught henceforth in our schools?"

Kurt Kiesinger, we hear, is personally immaculate, cultured, charming, a linguist, perfectly mannered, privately decent, a proud lover of his native Swabian soil. As a youth he wanted to become a German poet, and he still likes to recite classic Swabian verse, also Tocqueville. He claims to be able to speak today to simple folk and tomorrow, in the dean's place, to a student audience. To characterize his self-portraiture: when he was interviewed for American television he said that a deNazification court had not only acquitted him but praised him for valiant service to the anti-Nazi cause and for taking great risks in the process. I found no such remark of his quoted in any German paper, and in the American interview he cautiously refrained from personal assertions of valor and risk, citing only the deNazification verdict.

Many Germans—not all of them, probably just a small minority, perhaps a million—are in dismay. Chancellor Kiesinger attests a change that antedates his election; but now the moment has come. What seemed impossible ten years ago has become a fact almost without resistance. That former Nazis were going to occupy high posts, even political posts, was virtually unavoidable; there simply were not enough non-Nazis to run our government, our economy, our educational system. No objections were raised when Kiesinger became prime minister in Baden-Württemberg. But the federal chancellery is something else again. That a former Nazi is now governing the Federal Republic means that henceforth a Nazi past will not matter.

It is argued that if a man joined the Nazis in 1933 but came to see the error of his ways—if the atrocities of the regime shocked him into resisting inwardly, though not outwardly, and he rendered yeoman service in the reconstruction after 1945—a mistake made decades ago should be balanced against his later probation.

I differ in only one point, but in the crucial one: that joining the Nazis in 1933 was "a mistake." Mistake or moral collapse: that is the question.

All of us who were adults in 1933 have our memories. Talks in those days were revealing. Few indeed saw clearly and judged uncompromisingly; yet one did not need to feel alone. We felt that we, this million or so, were Germany. If a man would not put the Jewish question first ("Let's leave the Jewish question aside for once," I used to hear from perfectly decent people) the Reichstag fire told him what was going on. But I remember how a friend of mine relished the cunning which the Nazis showed on that occasion.

The experience has made distrust among us unavoidable. Every first look at a fellow German will raise the same questions: Who are you really? What lies behind your façade? What may come out of you? What can I trust in?

Those who lack the experience, who have not witnessed the

self-exposure of people they had regarded as rational persons, as friends—those who have not actually seen the walls go up between us will find it hard to understand in retrospect. And of the knowing, of the guilty, far too many will now shroud and, if possible, withhold the knowledge from anyone who was then young or unborn. They will not admit that the state which came into being in 1933 was criminal. They want a statute of limitations. They want to "conquer the past," which is impossible. It was all "a mistake."

But it was much more. It was a breakdown—or a revelation—of the character of a German majority. Considering the facts that everyone could see, it was possible only if one would either deny the facts or treat them as nonexistent. It took criminal untruthfulness. To fail to be absolutely, unreservedly anti-Nazi in view of the criminal facts, one had to be unimpressed by lawlessness and crime wherever apparent. Without profound inhumanity it was not possible.

Of course, this is only the position of that small minority, of the few who think truthfully and will not qualify facts. The fact that their state, their republic, is now represented by a former Nazi frightens them because once more, as frequently in Prussian and German history, they must feel excluded. Kiesinger seems not to care about their judgment, though it will hang over him in times to come.

Let me quote now from Grass's letter to Brandt:

Before you, between Messrs. Kiesinger and Strauss, have to turn state's evidence on behalf of a false harmony, I beg you once more to consider the incalculable consequences of such a decision. . . . How are we to continue defending the Social Democratic Party as an alternative when the proportional mélange of the grand coalition has made the profile of a Willy Brandt unrecognizable? Universal adjustment will be the rule of political and social conduct. But the youth of our country will turn away from the state and its constitution. . . .

What happened was astounding. The new state came about quite peacefully, without police or military force and without threats to anyone's private existence, and Germans bereft of political insight accordingly consider it a democracy of the kind we used to have. But it is a dictatorship, not by the military but by politicians—a notion probably never yet put into practice, except perhaps by the Austrian post–World War II prototype of a grand coalition. It acts as if it had a unifying program, whereas in fact it merely scrambles many views. It rules by confusion. And the ruling oligarchy does not rest on a tradition of old families but on a haphazard mass of tradition-less politicians.

What holds them together? What is their coalition based upon? The people had no hand in its establishment. But the respect that will be paid at once to any government of ours became apparent after my first criticisms, when I was told that I had no right to attack a man who had, after all, been "elected." Elected? Yes, by the clique of party bosses who arranged this deal. Is the horse-trading of a small clique to be called an "election"?

Political scientists have been given a new research object. What form of government does this new regime constitute? One may say that ultimately it rests on a popular vote, and what happens later will in due time also be determined by voters choosing between parties—so democracy is continuing, however odd its transient form may appear. But it remains to be seen what our "elected" dictators will decide and do in the interim, and whether some now unforeseeable acts will not prevent us from voting them out again.

Do they have any other aims at all? As yet there are no signs of any joint, comprehensive political program.

There is talk of electoral reform, but that would have to be preceded by difficult investigations, since no one really knows how the candidates on our party lists are picked in fact.

There is talk of budgetary reform; but nothing indicates that the new men will attack the root of the evil: fiscal dishonesty. Presumably they will be satisfied with bridging short-range "gaps."

Now and then somebody mentions the emergency laws, the gravest past and future threat to our republic. We have reason to fear that in this one point the coalition will use its omnipotence to pass the laws.

Kiesinger let it be known that his ministers would need cabinet approval for political speeches or interviews—a popular step, since the loquacity of our politicians had become intolerable. At the same time, however, it is a step toward the secrecy which any oligarchy needs to be secure.

And the gentlemen will not be silencing each other so as to revitalize our parliament, the proper forum for enlightening and moving great debates. On the contrary. Presaging the Bundestag's reduction to a decorative shadow existence, it has already been asked to grant the government blanket authority to raise or cut taxes up to 10 per cent without parliamentary approval. The road we have taken with this regime is obvious.

Will the grand coalition accomplish the purpose of the bipartisan oligarchy? Will it terminate opposition in the Federal Republic?

The formal possibility of further parliamentary opposition rests with an infinitesimal group, the Free Democrats. They can speak up on the floor of the Bundestag, but they do not count—first, because of their impotence, and second, because they convince no one, have changed sides too often, and have no political goal except to survive as a party.

We had a case of intraparty opposition: the revolt of rank-and-file Social Democrats against the leadership's course. It seems to have been quite an event, credible and symbolized by the stand which Brandt's son took against his father. But in a matter of weeks the uprising folded. The Social Democrats are the best organized, most thoroughly institutionalized German party; they pride themselves on their internal democracy; but party officials have their own pride, and each one will see his own position jeopardized by any threat to the unity of the party. A split could not but improve the political climate in the country at large. More seriousness and more vitality would be inevitable if a large part of German Social Democracy managed to break away. But this is most unlikely and may be impossible.

Finally, the opposition to all other parties has now assumed the form of a new one, a party based on the ancient and yet ever-modern nationalist mentality. The "National Democrats" have grown swiftly in membership and voting strength. They have overcome the "5 per cent clause," the oligarchy's defense mechanism against new parties, and have invaded several state legislatures. Indications are that they will keep growing and will enter the Bundestag in force after the next election. There is mounting concern in all other parties; the public worries about the resurgence of nationalism, and some fear the worst. Abroad the new group is already known as "the neo-Nazi party."

It does represent an old and silly cause which today seems to border on madness. And yet, I cannot get excited about the platitudes these people are declaiming on so low a level.

In no event can this be called the birth or rebirth of a Hitler type of Nazism. The National Democrats have no private army. They do not organize a state within the state that might fill every post at the moment of seizing power. Their posture is not that of an ideological movement claiming and absorbing the whole human being. They lack the desperadoes of the early thirties, the host of men uprooted by World War I and its aftermath, tied to nothing, ready for anything, who came on the scene in those days with vigor and calculating shrewdness and sometimes superior intelligence, and with the gift of recognizing real power and making it serve their ends. The new party is a party among others. It is not totalitarian. There was more to Nazism than spouting Nazi phrases and attracting old Nazis, malcontents, and the confused young.

Yet why is the party effective? It is because it exudes something like a faith, and the voters want a faith. They want something to believe in, something they feel they live for, something to warm the heart. A party that represents no special interest satisfies the longing for credibility, the point in which all other parties fail. The new opposition is a product of the other parties, and it would be gratifying if it brought them back to reason now that their alliance has stripped them of every shred of trustworthiness. The new party reveals the bankruptcy of the rest.

It is quite true that its intellectual sterility, its type of representation, and its trite vocabulary will not let it make an impression except on its own level; but at the moment the subjective power of an underlying faith gives it a dangerous edge. Since our parties, our politicians, our governments lack any political faith, since all they stand for is the German void, people have no faith in them either. Since no new state emerged in 1945, all hopes and expectations notwithstanding, there seems to be no replenishing the void. The craziest faith may spread in such a situation. The impulses behind the National Democratic Party have no great original dynamism nowadays, but where there is no dynamic impulse at all the most trivial one may suddenly be energized and flare up like a match in the darkness.

Let us not deceive ourselves about current German nationalism. Throughout our population I can see no serious nationalist surge. The danger is not nationalism but the lack of something to believe in. Neonationalism can thrive only because there is nothing else.

Nor can the blame for the new nationalist wave be placed

solely or even primarily on the Federal Republic. I cannot forget what a prominent German politician said to me in 1958 or 1959: "For ten years we have been glorifying Europe to the German people. Were the Germans not about to become Europeans and to bear themselves as Europeans, truthfully and earnestly and in good faith? And now the British and French go in for nationalism. How can we help going along?"

The Federal Republic went along, and having done so, it naturally assumed all the specific hues of past German nationalism.

In 1945 we wanted to build on the idea of freedom, to organize ourselves in a democracy under a republican form of government. We failed. We are regressing farther and farther. The last twenty years have shown that the Germans have not changed. The new party's spirit can pervade everything now, our army and our bureaucracy, our everyday language and our other parties which will adopt it when it comes back into fashion. It exists everywhere and needs only to be encouraged.

I consider it very cheap to be outraged at the new party, and idle to try arguing against the nuisance. Our politicians should ask themselves why it succeeds. They are the cause. The new party could not exist without the political climate of the Federal Republic, and the one way to combat it is for our major parties to develop credibility and substance.

If we take recent events for the first symptoms of a future condition we may anticipate a change in the meaning of opposition as such. It is conceivable that soon there will be no more opposition as we understand it. As a matter of form, then, "opposition" will mean "talking as if," and as a matter of fact it will be a mere function in the opportunistic bustle of a pointlessly embroiled multitude. Issues will be changeable at will. Having fought for no cause, having kept no faith, yesterday's deadly enemies will get along as if nothing had happened. Augur will laugh at augur; neither will respect the other or himself. No one will trust anyone or deserve anyone's trust. Since no man will take a position, none will be in opposition.

Opposition may cease. Much of it is curiously ambiguous even now. A glance at the prospects of opposition in our republic in the years ahead may well dishearten us. Yet this only adds to the challenge for every German to make it clear to himself what he wants and whether he wants anything at all—whether he will participate in that empty activity of aimless contention or will yield to resignation, abandon political hope, and withdraw in silence to another world.

But if we want to live, if we want to be ourselves, we must not despair. This applies to everything I say in this book. We can go our way with those who will at least struggle for the possibility of reason and preserve human dignity. There is always a chance that ultimately man will conquer the unreason in himself; if not, he will have the alibi, so to speak, of having set another course that failed. Unconsciously or consciously, each individual chooses how he wants to live, to think, to act, and to die.